Python 2 and 3 Compatibility

With Six and Python-Future Libraries

Joannah Nanjekye

Apress®

Python 2 and 3 Compatibility

Joannah Nanjekye
Kampala, Uganda

ISBN-13 (pbk): 978-1-4842-2954-5   ISBN-13 (electronic): 978-1-4842-2955-2
https://doi.org/10.1007/978-1-4842-2955-2

Library of Congress Control Number: 2017962338

Cover image designed by Freepik

Managing Director: Welmoed Spahr
Editorial Director: Todd Green
Acquisitions Editor: Todd Green
Development Editor: James Markham
Technical Reviewer: Benjamin Peterson
Coordinating Editor: Jill Balzano
Copy Editor: Kim Burton-Weisman
Compositor: SPi Global
Indexer: SPi Global
Artist: SPi Global

Distributed to the book trade worldwide by Springer Science+Business Media New York, 233 Spring Street, 6th Floor, New York, NY 10013. Phone 1-800-SPRINGER, fax (201) 348-4505, e-mail orders-ny@springer-sbm.com, or visit www.springeronline.com. Apress Media, LLC is a California LLC and the sole member (owner) is Springer Science + Business Media Finance Inc (SSBM Finance Inc). SSBM Finance Inc is a **Delaware** corporation.

For information on translations, please e-mail rights@apress.com, or visit http://www.apress.com/rights-permissions.

Apress titles may be purchased in bulk for academic, corporate, or promotional use. eBook versions and licenses are also available for most titles. For more information, reference our Print and eBook Bulk Sales web page at http://www.apress.com/bulk-sales.

Any source code or other supplementary material referenced by the author in this book is available to readers on GitHub via the book's product page, located at www.apress.com/9781484229545. For more detailed information, please visit http://www.apress.com/source-code.

Printed on acid-free paper

To my family, who have always given me the support to soar; most importantly, my mother, who always reminds me that one of the best decisions I have ever made was to become an engineer. I am grateful for the all-around support (Internet, food, and everything I can't list here because of space).

To the hardworking chief forensic accountant without a CPA, Edmond Mabinda, who tracks every penny in Uganda—other than his own.
Thanks for your work on this and the work you will continue doing.

I'm not forgetting Phionah Bugosi, the programmer who cares more about the color of her laptop bag than her code. Thanks for your work reviewing all the code.

Contents

About the Author

Joannah Nanjekye is from Uganda. She is a software engineer, a conference speaker, and an open source contributor. She has spoken at PyCon ZA in South Africa in 2016 and 2017, and at other Python meetups. She shares her implementation knowledge of Python 2 and 3 support from experiences with open source projects. She worked as a software developer for Laboremus Uganda and Fintech Uganda before pursuing a career as an aeronautical engineer with a focus on avionics at Kenya Aeronautical College. She is a proud alum of Outreachy and Rails Girls Summer of Code, where she learned most of the engineering skills. She is also proud of her working with qutebrowser and Ceph.

About the Technical Reviewer

Benjamin Peterson is a core developer of CPython and PyPy. He wrote the six Python 2&3 compatibility library.

Acknowledgments

Writing a technical book comes later on in one's career. I therefore admit that I have learned from a lot of experiences. I am sharing a subset of these experiences in this book.

First, I would like to thank Wilson Kigundu for the email that always keeps me hoping for a brighter future in my engineering career, sent at a time when my first strike into engineering felt like a blander of the century at the time.

I share content drawing from my experiences as an open source contributor, and as such, I would love to thank the open source mentors that I have worked with on qutebrowser and Ceph. I thank Florian Bruhin for all the guidance he accorded when I worked with Keziah on qutebrowser during Rails Girls Summer of Code. Most of the Python and Git that I know, I learned from working on qutebrowser. I also thank Ali Maredia, a mentor from Ceph that sacrificed his time, especially his lunch time, to mentor me on object storage, Ceph, and working with Amazon Web Services during my outreachy internship. I am very proud of my work and what I learned during this internship.

I also take this opportunity to thank the editors I worked with on my end, but also on the Apress side. Thank you Sandra Nabwire, Lynn Kirabo for your editorial work. Special thanks to the technical editors Ed Schofield (on my end) and Benjamin Peterson (from Apress) for the guidance. Great thanks to Jill Balzano and James Markham for making this book more than a success.

Lastly, I would love to thank Paul Bagyenda, my first university programming lecturer that taught me a lesson in persistence. Your Python programming class was one of the hardest, but looking back, I think you taught real programming. If anything, you made me who I am today. You had to appear in my first book.

Introduction

All of our Python eggs supported in a unified code basket

Python 2 and 3 compatibility has been discussed in many Python gatherings, especially as we approach the Python 2 End Of Life (EOL). It is much more than a topic making news in the community.

The Python project started in 1980 as a work by the "Benevolent Dictator For Life" Guido Van Rossum, who continues to be commander-in-chief in terms of giving direction to the Python language. In October 2000, Python 2.0 was released with many prime features; its implementation became public and community backed. In December 2008, a backward-incompatible Python 3 (a.k.a. Python 3K and Python 3000) was released; after rigorous testing, it was backported in the backward-compatible Python 2.6.x and Python 2.7.x versions.

Python 3 was built to improve significant design shortcomings in the language. There are features in which improvements did not play well with backward compatibility, and therefore needed a new major version number. It removed feature duplication in duplicative constructs and modules while still providing for a multiparadigm language in ways that are more obvious than they were in Python 2.x. It is very accurate to say that you are better off using and supporting Python 3.

To assume that all Python users will immediately switch to Python 3 is not very wise, however, even though the Python 2 EOL date was postponed to 2020. Despite some discomfort in the Python community, Python 2.7 will be supported for some time. It is clear that Python 3 is the future.

We have a future that is purely Python 3 and a present with Python 2 still in use; therefore, current support for both versions is the best remedy—especially for developers building libraries and tools, and anyone building a system that depends on Python.

Much like going on a diet, the transition is not fun, however beneficial it may be. There is a large contrast when you know you have to do something in which the process is sacrificial but the end justifies the means. The only question asked is whether you would rather stay where you are or persevere your way to a better place.

Python 3.0 broke compatibility and a sizable portion of Python 2 code does not run in Python 3 unless it is converted. Some people looked at Python 3 as the blander of the Century. Changes to Python's dynamic typing and the semantics in methods for dictionaries make the translation from Python 2.x to Python 3.x very difficult.

2to3 is one of the quick fixes to translate Python 2 code to Python 3; however, it is not a recommended practice. The clean and tested way is to write a single code base that is capable of running reliably in both Python 2 and 3, using compatibility modules such as Python-future and six.

The following are some of the reasons why you want to support both Python 2 and Python 3:

- The upcoming Python 2 EOL. The exact date has not been determined, but rumor has it that it will be in 2020 around time for Pycon in the US. You do not want to be caught unaware.

- Perhaps you have Python 2 users using your system or library, but you want to prepare for the future, which is evidently Python 3. The only option you have is to ensure that your system or library executes reliably in both versions.

- You're not ready to entirely port to Python 3. Always choose neutral compatibility. It is the safest.

This book unfolds the concepts you need to know to achieve Python 2 and 3 compatibility.

About this Book

This book explains the magic of Python 2 and Python 3 compatibility in a unified code base in 12 detailed chapters. You will work on tasks with an open source mentor (who I will introduce later):

- Printing is the most known difference between Python 2 and 3. Chapter 1 explains how to write the `print` statement as a function—instead with the helper modules—to achieve neutral compatibility. Backtick repr is also discussed.

- There is also contrast with number operations and representations. Chapter 2 explains how to provide Python 2 and 3 compatibility with long integers, inspecting integers, and division. It also looks at compatibility with octal literals, commonly known as octal constants.

- Chapter 3 discusses how to write metaclasses that stand the Python 2 and 3 syntax storms by using six and Python-future.

- Python 3 strings are Unicode. The `unicode()` function in Python 2 is long gone. Chapter 4 goes into the detail about how to make peace between the Python 2 and 3 differences in Unicode string literals, base strings, byte string literals, and string IO.

- Chapter 5 explains how to handle imports relative (or not) to a package to ensure Python 2 and Python 3 compatibility.

- Chapter 6 explains how to write code to handle raising exceptions, catching exceptions, and exception chaining that will execute reliably in Python 2 and Python 3.

- HTML processing in a single Python neutral code base is explained in Chapter 7, which also covers HTML parsing and escaping.

- Chapter 8 discusses how to achieve Python neutral compatibility when using the `file()` procedure and the FileIO operations.

- Chapter 9 explores custom class behavior in a few methods. Syntactical differences and common syntax that can lead to compatibility in both Python 2 and 3 are explained.

- Neutral compatibility for collections and iterators is discussed with clear examples in Chapter 10. Operations on dictionaries are also explained.

- Other built-in neutral compatibility concepts, such as the `cmp`, `chr`, and `reload` functions are explained in Chapter 11.

- Chapter 12 discusses concepts on how to write a unified code base for standard library modules that had a name change or changed in other ways.

Conventions

This book uses the term *Python neutral compatibility* to refer to the state where a given piece of Python code is capable of running without any errors or bugs in both Python 2 and 3.

Throughout this book, I use some code extracted directly from open source projects, and edited in some cases, but also my own code to clearly illustrate the concepts. Some of the code snippets do not execute because they are partial extracts from an open source project for purposes of explaining the concepts.

Tasks

This book features tasks being worked on by a developer and his mentor. All the tasks have solutions, but it is recommended that you try out the task before looking ahead at the solution. This will be more rewarding and fun to you.

Python Versions

If you have been around the Python ecosystem, you may have noticed that it is continuously evolving and new versions of Python are being released. This is why we are even discussing compatibility. However, you may try a piece of code from this book in a particular Python version and it fails. This should not be very common, however; and if it does happen, do not burn the book or stop reading it.

I used Python 3.5 and 2.7 to test all the examples in this book. If you find your version failing, you can let me know through Apress so that we can rectify this in another edition.

About You

Python neutral compatibility is considered an advanced topic for many people. You need to have worked with Python enough to appreciate why the differences in the versions are a big deal. If you have only worked with either Python 2 or Python 3, that is fine; there is an entire section of this book about the differences between Python 2 and 3.

But if you do not have any Python knowledge, you may be better off taking a Python tutorial. If you are unsure of your skills, then take a simple test. How do you loop over a range of numbers? If you thought of the range function, then you know enough Python to follow this book. But if you did not, then you probably want to consider the tutorial path.

Are you on board? Amazing! Let's start with a little foundation.

Contrasts Between Python 2 and Python 3

Before we look at the concepts of writing a single code base that executes reliably in both Python 2 and Python 3, let's explore the programmatic differences between the two to appreciate their contrast.

Print

Print is a built-in function in Python 3 and no longer a statement. This is probably the most popularly known contrast, but it's worth discussing. The Python 2 `print` statement was replaced with a `print()` function. The content to print should be placed in the parentheses.

```
Python 2

print "I am an Engineer",              #suppress newline
print "I was born one"

Python 3

print ("I am an Engineer", end=" ")    #suppress newline
print ("I was born one")
```

To suppress a newline in Python 2, we append a comma at the end of the statement; whereas in Python 3, the syntax requires using the end keyword argument, which defines the final character printed (the default is a newline).

Division

In Python 3, a single slash results in a floating point number and double slashes for integer divisions. In contrast, Python 2 uses a single slash to return both integer and floating numbers, depending on the type of the numbers involved.

```
Python 2

4/3 = 1

4.0/3 = 1.3333333

Python 3

4//3 = 1

4 / 3 = 1.333333
```

Input

The raw_input() function in Python 2 works the same way as the input() function in Python 3 . They both return user input as a string. They must be converted if there is need for a different type. The eval() method can be used to get user input as some type other than a string; but this is not recommended. Instead, casting the user input to a type of choice is recommended.

```
Python 2

my_input = raw_input()              # my_input is of type string
my_input = float(raw_input())       # my_input is of type float
my_input = int(raw_input())         # my_input is of type integer

Python 3

my_input = input()                  # my_input is of type string
my_input = float(input())           # my_input is of type float
my_input = int(input())             # my_input is of type integer

my_input = eval(input())            # Not recommended
```

Files

The name of the function used to open a file was changed. The file() function was removed in Python 3. It was replaced with the open() function.

```
Python 2

myFile = file("my_file.txt")

Python 3

myFile = open("my_file.txt",'r')
```

Range

The range() function in Python 2 works the same ways as the xrange() function in Python 3. It does not return a list and can handle considerably large values.

```
Python 2

L = range(10)                    # L is [0,1,2,3,4,5,6,7,8,9]

Python 3

L = list(range(10))              # L is [0,1,2,3,4,5,6,7,8,9]

# The following causes an error in Python 2 but is valid in Python 3

for i in range(1000000000000)
```

Strings

By default, Python 2.x uses the ASCII alphabet, which is limited to hundreds of characters in extended forms, and it is not as flexible in encoding, especially with non-English characters. To use Unicode character encoding, with more characters and historic scripts and symbol sets, use the *u* prefix.

Python 3 uses Unicode characters by default, which saves lots of time in development because Unicode supports greater linguistic diversity.

The unicode() function was removed in Python 3 because all strings in Python 3 are Unicode; whereas to make a string unicode in Python 2, you either use the unicode() function or prepend the string with u.

```
Python 2

my_string = "hello world "
s = unicode( string)
s = u"\u20AC"
s = ur"\w"

Python 2

my_string = 2
s = str( string)
s = "\u20AC"
s = r"\w"
```

Raising Exceptions

The new syntax for raising exceptions requires us to enclose the exception argument in parentheses, whereas the old syntax doesn't.

Python 2

```
raise ValueError, "dodgy value"

# exceptions with traceback
traceback = sys.exec_info()[2]
raise ValueError, "dodgy value", traceback
```

Python 3

```
raise ValueError("dodgy value")

# exceptions with traceback
raise ValueError("dodgy value").with_traceback()
```

Python 2 accepts both the old and new syntax for raising exceptions; however, Python 3 will loudly shout at an exception by raising a syntax error if the old syntax is used.

Handling Exceptions

The Python 2 way of handling exceptions changed and now requires the use of the as keyword.

Python 2

```
try:

except NameError, e:
```

Python 3

```
try:

except NameError as e:
```

These are only a few of the changes that came with Python 3. The focus of this book is not to explain the differences between the Python versions. Detailed explanations and concepts shall be discussed in the neutral compatibility chapters later in this book.

Compatibility Modules

Python-future, six, and __future__ are modules that help us achieve Python 2 and Python 3 compatibility. They provide utilities that help us write code that is compatible with both Python 2 and Python 3. They are intended for code bases that run unmodified in both Python 2 and Python 3.

Some library developers have provided Python 2 and Python 3 support for their libraries by using constructs such as this:

```
if sys.version_info[0] == 2:
    # Python 2 code
else:
    # Python 3 code
```

In places where there are differences between Python 2 and Python 3, however, the __future__, Python-future and six libraries provide wrappers that help you write a single and clean neutral code base.

__future__

__future__ is a real module built into Python to help with compatibility. To implement neutral compatibility in Python 3 and 2, we need to import this built-in module and any relevant Python-future or six packages. The __future__ module allows us to activate new Python language features that are not compatible with the current interpreter version.

Any __future__ import must appear at the top of the module; anything contrary causes a grave syntax error. All other imports, including Python-future and six imports, must appear below __future__ imports and before any other import.

This is correct:

```
from __future__ import print_function
from builtins import str
```

This is not correct:

```
from django.conf.urls import url
from . import views
from builtins import str
from __future__ import print_function
```

Let's look at how the following Python 2 script can be changed to run in both Python 2 and Python 3 by using the built in __future__ module.

Download Introduction/isogram.py

```
def is_isogram(word):
    if len(word) == 0:
        word_tuple = (word, False)
        print word_tuple
    elif not isinstance(word, str):
        word_tuple = (word, False)
        raise TypeError("Argument should be a string")
    else:
        if len(word) == len(set(word)):
                word_tuple = (word, True)
                print word_tuple
```

```
        else:
                word_tuple = (word, False)
                print word_tuple

is_isogram("abolishment")
```

The preceding is a simple script with only one thing that prevents it from executing correctly in Python 3: the print statement. We therefore need to change the print statement to a print function. But first, we need a __future__ import with a relevant print_function module to allow us use the print function feature that does not exist in Python 2. The following is a new script that executes correctly in Python 2.x and Python 3.x.

Download Introduction/compatible_isogram.py

```
from __future__ import print_function

def is_isogram(word):
    if len(word) == 0:
        word_tuple = (word, False)
        print (word_tuple)
    elif not isinstance(word, str):
        word_tuple = (word, False)
        raise TypeError("Argument should be a string")
    else:
        if len(word) == len(set(word)):
                word_tuple = (word, True)
                print (word_tuple)
        else:
                word_tuple = (word, False)
                print (word_tuple)

is_isogram("abolishment")
```

Python-future

Python-future is a compatibility tier between Python 2.x and 3.x. It enables us to write a single Python 3.x code base that runs reliably in Python 2.x with fewer outlays.

Python-future has packages that provide forward- and backward-porting features for Python 2.x and Python 3.x. In addition, it offers futurize and pasteurize, which aid in easily changing a Python 2.x or Python 3.x code base to support both Python 2 and 3 in a sole Python 3 code base.

Futurize Package

As stated earlier, Python-future comes with a futurize package that takes Python 2 code into a series of magical fixes that convert into pure Python 3 code. It automatically adds __future__ and future package imports at the top of the module to allow the code to run in Python 2. Take a look at the following example of the Python 2 code:

Download Introduction/remove_duplicate.py

```python
def remove_duplicates(string):
        if string.isalpha():
        new_string = set(string)                        #sets have no duplicates
        duplicates_count = len(string) - len(new_string)
        final_string = sorted( list(new_string))
        unique_string   = ''.join(final_string)
        print unique_string, duplicates_count
        else :
        print 'Argument should be a string'

print "Give me a string:",
given_str = raw_input()
remove_duplicates(given_str)
```

If we run futurize -w remove_duplicate.py, we get a converted version of the preceding code that is able to execute correctly in both Python 2.x and Python 3.x. This results in the following code.

Download Introduction/compatible_remove_duplicate.py

```python
from __future__ import print_function
from future import standard_library
standard_library.install_aliases()
from builtins import input

def remove_duplicates(string):
        if string.isalpha():
        new_string = set(string)                        #sets have no duplicates
        duplicates_count = len(string) - len(new_string)
        final_string = sorted( list(new_string))
        unique_string   = ''.join(final_string)
        print (unique_string, duplicates_count)
        else :
        print ('Argument should be a string')

print ('Give me a string:',end=' ')
given_str = input()
remove_duplicates(given_str)
```

Past Package

The past package has the ability to automatically translate relatively non-complex Python 2 modules to Python 3 on import. It can be used in a real-world module; for example, it may be from the Python Package Index (PyPI) or any other module that has not been ported to work in Python 3.

Let's assume that we want to use the Asynchronous Component-based Event Application Framework from PyPI, but it is not yet ported. First, we need to install it using

```
Pip install circuit
```

Then, we pass the module name to the autotranslate() function.

```
$ python3

>>> from past import autotranslate
>>> autotranslate(['circuit'])
>>> import circuit
```

This automatically translates and runs the circuit module and any submodules in the circuit package. It gives you the ability to use Python 3 without the need for all of your dependencies supporting Python 3. It should be used sparingly and with caution. The recommended way is to provide Python 2 and Python 3 compatibility to the Python 2–dependent modules in a single code base and push changes to the upstream project.

Python-future vs. six

Python-future and six both enable us write code that runs unmodified in Python 2 and Python 3.

Python-future has an advantage over six: it allows standard Py3 code to run with almost no modification in both Python 3 and Python 2. It also makes it possible to write a single-source code base that works in both Python 2 and Python 3.

The real advantage of six is for libraries, where it is a small dependency. Python-future's backported types are a disadvantage for libraries, where they could "leak" out to calling code if not used carefully.

six is recommended when you need to support both versions. Python-future is preferred when you need a clean upgrade path. Note that the fewer dependencies in your code, the better.

In this book, I give unbiased details on the usage of both libraries so that you are comfortable using whichever you choose.

six

Like Python-future, six is a Python compatibility library. It contains features that help you work around the differences in Python versions. The aim of six is to help you write code that is capable of running in both Python 2.x and 3.x. six has Python support from version 2.6. It is easy to integrate into your project because it contains just a single file.

The following is an example of the six module. First, it needs to be imported.

```
Download Introduction/dispatch_types.py
```

```
import six

def dispatch_types(value):
    if isinstance(value, six.integer_types):
        handle_integer(value)
    elif isinstance(value, six.class_types):
        handle_class(value)
    elif isinstance(value, six.string_types):
        handle_string(value)
```

There are complex scenarios where we need to use the type of if statement shown earlier. The six package makes this simple by providing PY2 and PY3 boolean constants.

```
if six.PY2:
    # Python 2 code
else:
    # Python 3 code
```

> **Note** You may import six and Python-future after other module imports, but __future__ is special, and it must be imported before other modules.

Which Python Versions to Support

If you decide to use Python-future, then you will only be able to support Python 2.6 + and Python 3.3 +. If you need to support older versions, six allows you to support Python 2.4 and onward.

> **Note** The built-in __future__ module also helps us achieve compatibility. Minimize the use of third-party modules wherever the built-in module is sufficient.

Setup

To follow the examples in this book, you need to install both Python 2 and Python 3. More information on this is available on the Python documentation (https://www.python.org).

We will use pip to install the Python-future and six compatibility libraries.

This installs Python-future:

```
pip install future
```

This installs six:

```
pip install six
```

Are you ready? Let's begin our take-off run!

## CHAPTER 1

Printing and Backtick repr

Printing is the most well-known difference between Python 2 and Python 3. The print statement in Python 2 does not require parentheses; it is a function in Python 3. There is also a difference in the backtick repr. This chapter discusses the polarities of these features between the Python versions and the techniques to achieve their compatibility.

Print

As discussed in this book's introduction, the print statement in Python 2 became a function in Python 3, which means that we have to wrap the content that we want to print within parentheses. Before we start converting some scripts, let me explain a few "yang"s to the print neutral compatibility "yin" using the __future__ and the six modules.

Using __future__

__future__ is a built-in module that features compatibility modules. For any modules with print statements in Python 2, you must use the __future__ import followed by the print_function module in the first line of code in the file.

```
from __future__ print_function
```

Then use the function form; print("something") whenever the print statement is used.
The following Python 2 code

```
Download Print/py2_print.py
```

```
Import sys

print >> sys.stderr, 'echo Lima golf'
print 'say again'
print  'I say again', 'echo Lima golf'
print  'Roger',
```

becomes

Download Print/future_print.py

```
from __future__ import print_function
import sys

print('echo lima golf', file=sys.stderr)
print ('say again')
print ('I say again', 'echo lima golf')
print ( 'Roger', end='')
```

In Python 2, the print function with one argument prints a given string in the argument. With multiple strings, if we do not import print_function to override Python 2 behavior, a tuple prints. If we want to print a tuple using the Python 3 syntax, then we need to use more parentheses.

```
# this prints a tuple in Python 2 if print_function is not imported
print ('I say again', 'echo Lima golf')

#prints a tuple in Python 3
print (('I say again', 'echo Lima golf')).
```

To print a tuple in Python 3, use double parentheses, as shown in the preceding code. Let's now see how we can use six to maintain compatibility with the print function.

Using six

The following is used with any modules with print statements, and with any modules where you use the six import to access the wrapper print function that helps you achieve neutral Python compatibility:

```
import six
```

Then use the six.print_(*args, *, file=sys.stdout, end="\n", sep=" ", flush=False) function as a wrapper to the print syntactical differences between Python 2 and Python 3.

The following Python 2 print statements

Download Print/py2_print.py

```
import sys

print >> sys.stderr, 'echo lima golf'
print 'say again'
print 'I say again', 'echo lima golf'
print 'Roger'
```

become

Download Print/six_print.py

```
import six
import sys
```

```
six.print_('echo lima golf', file=sys.stderr)
six.print_('say again')
six.print_('I say again', 'echo lima golf')
six.print_('Roger', file=sys.stdout, end='')
```

The function prints the arguments separated by sep. end is written after the last argument is printed. If flush is true, file.flush() is called after all data is written.

Use __future__ to avoid introducing many dependencies.

■ **Note**   You may import six and future after other module imports. __future__ is special and must be imported first.

Task: Introducing Your Mentor

Let me introduce you to Ali, a Red Hat engineer and the open source mentor that you will be working with on these interesting tasks. He is a good guy, by the way. The maintainers of the QEMU project told him that some Python scripts in the project only support Python 2. This is your first task. Ali informs you that you are going to work on only the print statements in these two methods, because they are in the same module. Take a look.

```
Download Print/qmp.py

def cmd_obj(self, qmp_cmd):
        """
        Send a QMP command to the QMP Monitor.

        @param qmp_cmd: QMP command to be sent as a Python dict
        @return QMP response as a Python dict or None if the connection has
                been closed
        """
        if self._debug:
            print >>sys.stderr, "QMP:>>> %s" % qmp_cmd
        try:
            self.__sock.sendall(json.dumps(qmp_cmd))
        except socket.error as err:
            if err[0] == errno.EPIPE:
                return
            raise socket.error(err)
        resp = self.__json_read()
        if self._debug:
            print >>sys.stderr, "QMP:<<< %s" % resp
        return resp

def _execute_cmd(self, cmdline):
        if cmdline.split()[0] == "cpu":
                # trap the cpu command, it requires special setting
                try:
                idx = int(cmdline.split()[1])
```

```
                    if not 'return' in self.__cmd_passthrough('info version', idx):
                            print 'bad CPU index'
                            return True
                    self.__cpu_index = idx
                    except ValueError:
                    print 'cpu command takes an integer argument'
                    return True
        resp = self.__cmd_passthrough(cmdline, self.__cpu_index)
        if resp is None:
                    print 'Disconnected'
                    return False
        assert 'return' in resp or 'error' in resp
        if 'return' in resp:
                    # Success
                    if len(resp['return']) > 0:
                    print resp['return'],
        else:
                    # Error
                    print '%s: %s' % (resp['error']['class'], resp['error']['desc'])
        return True
```

"This is an easy one. Let's change the print statements to functions using both the __future__ and the six libraries," Ali says. After a few changes and reviews, the print statements in the methods are finally in shape. Let's take a look at what was merged.

Using __future__

All that was done was to import the print_function from __future__, and to keep the Python 3 syntax for it to work.

Download Print/future_qmp.py

```
from __future__ import print_function
import sys
def cmd_obj(self, qmp_cmd):
        """
        Send a QMP command to the QMP Monitor.

        @param qmp_cmd: QMP command to be sent as a Python dict
        @return QMP response as a Python dict or None if the connection has
                been closed
        """
        if self._debug:
                    print("QMP:>>> %s" % qmp_cmd, file=sys.stderr)
        try:
                    self.__sock.sendall((json.dumps(qmp_cmd)).encode('utf-8'))
        except socket.error as err:
                    if err[0] == errno.EPIPE:
                    return
                    raise
        resp = self.__json_read()
```

```python
        if self._debug:
                print("QMP:<<< %s" % resp, file=sys.stderr)
        return resp

def _execute_cmd(self, cmdline):
        if cmdline.split()[0] == "cpu":
                # trap the cpu command, it requires special setting
                try:
                idx = int(cmdline.split()[1])
                if not 'return' in self.__cmd_passthrough('info version', idx):
                        print ('bad CPU index')
                        return True
                self.__cpu_index = idx
                except ValueError:
                print ('cpu command takes an integer argument')
                return True
        resp = self.__cmd_passthrough(cmdline, self.__cpu_index)
        if resp is None:
                print ('Disconnected')
                return False
        assert 'return' in resp or 'error' in resp
        if 'return' in resp:
                # Success
                if len(resp['return']) > 0:
                print (resp['return'],  file=sys.stdout, end='')
        else:
                # Error
                print ('%s: %s' % (resp['error']['class'], resp['error']['desc']))
        return True
```

Using six

In six, we use the print_ wrapper function whenever there is a print statement, which "magically" works.

```python
Download Print/six_qmp.py

import six
import sys
def cmd_obj(self, qmp_cmd):
        """
        Send a QMP command to the QMP Monitor.

        @param qmp_cmd: QMP command to be sent as a Python dict
        @return QMP response as a Python dict or None if the connection has
                been closed
        """
        if self._debug:
                six.print_("QMP:>>> %s" % qmp_cmd, file=sys.stderr)
```

```python
    try:
            self.__sock.sendall((json.dumps(qmp_cmd)).encode('utf-8'))
    except socket.error as err:
            if err[0] == errno.EPIPE:
            return
            raise
    resp = self.__json_read()
    if self._debug:
            six.print_("QMP:<<< %s" % resp, file=sys.stderr)
    return resp

def _execute_cmd(self, cmdline):
    if cmdline.split()[0] == "cpu":
            # trap the cpu command, it requires special setting
            try:
            idx = int(cmdline.split()[1])
            if not 'return' in self.__cmd_passthrough('info version', idx):
                    six.print_ ('bad CPU index')
                    return True
            self.__cpu_index = idx
            except ValueError:
            six.print_ ('cpu command takes an integer argument')
            return True
    resp = self.__cmd_passthrough(cmdline, self.__cpu_index)
    if resp is None:
            six.print_ ('Disconnected')
            return False
    assert 'return' in resp or 'error' in resp
    if 'return' in resp:
            # Success
            if len(resp['return']) > 0:
            six.print_ (resp['return'],  file=sys.stdout, end='')
    else:
            # Error
            six.print_ ('%s: %s' % (resp['error']['class'], resp['error']['desc']))
    return True
```

You guys did well on the last patch. Your next task will be on backtick repr. But before I reveal the task, let me explain something about backtick repr.

Backtick repr

A *backtick* in Python is an operator that converts the contained expression into a string. A backtick is an alias to the repr() and str() methods because they all give the same results. The following is an example.

Download Print/backtick.py

```python
class backtick_example(object):
    def __repr__(self):
    return 'repr backtick_example'
```

```
    def __str__(self):
        return 'str backtick_example'

>>> a = backtick_example()

>>> repr(a)
#'repr backtick_example'

>>> `a`
#'repr backtick_example'

>>> str(a)
#'repr backtick_example'
```

Backticks have been deprecated and are not in Python 3, however. Instead, we use repr whenever there is need for backticks. Therefore, this code:

Download Print/qmp_print.py

```
def _print(self, qmp):
    indent = None
    if self._pretty:
        indent = 4
    jsobj = json.dumps(qmp, indent=indent)
    print `jsobj`
```

changes to:

Download Print/new_qmp_print.py

```
def _print(self, qmp):
    indent = None
    if self._pretty:
        indent = 4
    jsobj = json.dumps(qmp, indent=indent)
    print repr(jsobj)
```

for neutral compatibility in a single code base.

■ **Note**   We can achieve neutral compatibility without necessarily using a third-party module, because some constructs may have been deprecated, like in this example, or there is syntax that behaves the same in both Python 2 and 3. Where possible, reduce dependencies in your code.

Coexistence Gotchas

When attempting neutral compatibility for print statements, it is very easy to break code semantically as you make compatibility changes. Major examples of this are discussed in a later chapter of this book.

Before you embark on your coexistence project, you are required to have coverage tools that check that the code runs and gives same results in both Python versions.

You want unit tests in place to ensure that any incorrect change notifies you by a failing test.

Summary

We discussed the most common difference between Python 2 and Python 3, which is the print statement and backtick repr. For print statement compatibility, we can keep Python syntax by importing the print_ function from the built-in __future__ module, or we can use the print_ wrapper function from six. I also noted that backticks have been deprecated, so we should use repr whenever there is need for backticks.

TASK: PUTTING IT TOGETHER

You are tasked to work on the fuel-dev-tools-master project, in the astute.py source file in the fuel_dev_tools/docker directory. The task requires that the astute.py script run consistently on both Python 2 and Python 3.

Download Print/astute.py

```
def build_gem(self, source_dir):
    cmd = (
        'cd %(cwd)s && '
        'gem build %(gemspec)s'
    ) % {
    'cwd': source_dir,
    'gemspec': self.gemspec,
    }

    try:
        result = subprocess.check_output([
            cmd
        ], shell=True)

        self.print_debug(result)
    except subprocess.CalledProcessError as e:
        print 'GEM BUILD ERROR'
        error =`e.output`
        print error
        raise
```

Ali is already reaching you on IRC to discuss the new task. You quickly tell him that this time, you know what to do. After a little hacking, let's see what was merged. Fingers crossed to see if your changes make it in the merged patch.

Using six

The solution uses the print_ function from six. Therefore, instead of the print statement, use the six.print_() function.

Download Print/six_astute.py
```python
import six
def build_gem(self, source_dir):
    cmd = (
        'cd %(cwd)s && '
        'gem build %(gemspec)s'
    ) % {
    'cwd': source_dir,
    'gemspec': self.gemspec,
    }

    try:
        result = subprocess.check_output([
            cmd
        ], shell=True)

        self.print_debug(result)
    except subprocess.CalledProcessError as e:
        six.print_('GEM BUILD ERROR')
        error =repr(e.output)
        six.print_(error)
        Raise
```

Using future

The __future__ module solution only requires a single import of the print_function. It keeps the Python 3 syntax.

Download Print/future_astute.py
```python
from __future__ import print_function
def build_gem(self, source_dir):
    cmd = (
        'cd %(cwd)s && '
        'gem build %(gemspec)s'
    ) % {
    'cwd': source_dir,
    'gemspec': self.gemspec,
    }
    try:
        result = subprocess.check_output([
            cmd
        ], shell=True)
        self.print_debug(result)
```

```
except subprocess.CalledProcessError as e:
    print ('GEM BUILD ERROR')
    error =repr(e.output)
    print (error)
    raise
```

CHAPTER 2

Numbers

When implementing Python 2 and Python 3 compatibility in a single code base, division won't truncate unless double slashes are used, or __future__ importation to division is done. All integers are long; there are no short integers because long( ) is gone; octal constants must start with 0o (zero-oh); and there are syntax changes to note in the integer inspection. Let's discuss each of these in detail.

Inspecting Integers

In Python 3, there are no long integers; therefore, integer types are checked against type int; for example:

Download Numbers/inspectionpy3.py
```
y = 3
if isinstance(y, int):
    print ("y is an Integer")
else:
    print ("y is not an integer")
```

For compatibility with existing Python 2 code that still checks against the long type, Python-future offers a couple of options.

Using Python-future's builtins Module

Let's use int because it matches both int and long in Python 2.

Download Numbers/builtins_inspection.py
```
from builtins import int

y = 3
if isinstance(y, int):
    print ("y is an Integer")
else:
    print ("y is not an integer")
```

Using past.builtins from Python-future

Make use of the past.builtins modules from Python-future when doing integer inspection.

Download Numbers/past_inspection.py

```
from past.builtins import long

y = 3
if isinstance(y, (int, long)):
    print ("y is an Integer")
else:
    print ("y is not an integer")
```

We import long from past.builtins. We then check against both int and long because the number we want to check matches both int and long in Python 2 and only int in Python 3.

Using six

six provides an integer_types constant that differs between Python versions. The integer types in Python 2 are long and int, and in Python 3, it's only int.

Download Numbers/six_inspection.py

```
import six

y = 3
if isinstance(y, six.integer_types):
    print ("y is an Integer")
else:
    print ("y is not an integer")
```

Long Integers

In Python 3, long became int, and therefore are no short integers. For compatibility, we use int for both long and short integers; however, Python-future has a way out for this as well.

```
X = 9223389765478925808         # not x =  9223389765478925808L
```

Using Python-future's builtins Module

Here we make use of the builtins module to represent integers that work consistently in both Python 2 and Python 3.

Download Numbers/future_long.py

```
from builtins import int

longint = int(1)
```

Floor Division

Integer division, or *floor division*, is when the outcome of a division is rounded down. In Python 2, we use one forward slash to achieve integer division, as opposed to using double forward slashes in Python 3. For neutral compatibility, we use Python 3 division by using double forward slashes when dividing.

Download Numbers/integer_division.py

```
x, y = 5, 2

result = x // y

assert result == 2     # Not 2
```

Float Division

In true division, or *float division*, the outcome is not rounded down. In Python 2, we ensure one of the values is a float to achieve this, as opposed to using one forward slash in Python 3. Let's discuss how we can achieve neutral compatibility.

Using __future__

In a unified code base, we must use the __future__ import followed by the division module in the first line of code in the file (to achieve Python 3 behavior for float division by default).

Download Numbers/future_float_division.py

```
from __future__ import division    # this should be at the very top of the module

x, y = 5, 2

result = x / y

assert result == 2.5
```

Python 2 Compatible Division (Old Division)

Optionally, we can use the old division, which is compatible with Python 2 when using old_div from past.utils.

Using Python-future

Download Numbers/future_old_float_division.py

```
from past.utils import old_div     # this should be at the very top of the module

x, y = 5, 2

result = x / y

assert result == 1.25
```

Take a look at the following code.

Download Numbers/torrentparser.py

```
def parse_torrent_id(arg):
    torrent_id = None
  oct_lit = 0644
    if isinstance(arg, long):
        torrent_id = int(arg)
    elif isinstance(arg, float):
        torrent_id = int(arg)
        if torrent_id != arg:
            torrent_id = None
    else:
        try:
            torrent_id = int(arg)
            threshhold >= 6442450945
            if torrent_id >= threshhold / 2.0:
                torrent_id = None
            elif isinstance(torrent_id, float):
                torrent_id = threshhold / 2
        except (ValueError, TypeError):
            pass
        if torrent_id is None:
            try:
                int(arg, 16)
                torrent_id = arg
            except (ValueError, TypeError):
                pass
    return torrent_id, oct_lit
```

We defined a Python 2 parse_torrent_id method, which takes an arg argument and returns a tuple with two values: torrent_id and oct_lit. We performed integer division and true division on the variable threshold. Let's now look at converting this code to a format that can execute on both Python 2 and 3.

A quick scan reveals that this code has two known problems. First, it's inspecting the arg variable against the long type, which is not present in Python 3. Second, Python 3 has a different syntax for integer division and true division.

Using __future__

Download Numbers/future_torrentparser.py

```
from __future__ import division

def parse_torrent_id(arg):
    torrent_id = None
  oct_lit = 0644
    if isinstance(arg, int):
        torrent_id = int(arg)
    elif isinstance(arg, float):
        torrent_id = int(arg)
        if torrent_id != arg:
            torrent_id = None
```

```
    else:
        try:
            torrent_id = int(arg)
            if torrent_id >= 6442450945/ 2:
                torrent_id = None
            elif isinstance(torrent_id, float):
             torrent_id = threshhold // 2
        except (ValueError, TypeError):
            pass
        if torrent_id is None:
            try:
                int(arg, 16)
                torrent_id = arg
            except (ValueError, TypeError):
                pass
    return torrent_id, oct_lit
```

This solves the problem. First, we import the division module from the __future__ module to aid us in handling integer division compatibility. We can then use the Python 3 syntax, where true division uses two forward slashes, and integer division uses one forward slash.

You can also use six for the integer type inspections to achieve the same compatibility in this same piece of code.

Using six

Download Numbers/six_torrentparser.py

```
import six

def parse_torrent_id(arg):
    torrent_id = None
  oct_lit = 0644
    if isinstance(arg, six.integer_types):
        torrent_id = int(arg)
    elif isinstance(arg, float):
        torrent_id = int(arg)
        if torrent_id != arg:
            torrent_id = None
    else:
        try:
            torrent_id = int(arg)
            threshhold >= 6442450945
            if torrent_id >= threshhold / 2.0:
                torrent_id = None
            elif isinstance(torrent_id, float):
             torrent_id = threshhold // 2
        except (ValueError, TypeError):
            pass
```

```
    if torrent_id is None:
        try:
            int(arg, 16)
            torrent_id = arg
        except (ValueError, TypeError):
            pass
    return torrent_id, oct_lit
```

When using six, we still have to make one of the numbers a float in order to achieve true division in both Python 2 and 3. For integer inspection, check against its integer_types constant.

Running this code still gives errors. In Python 3, it complains about the lines with the oct_lit variable. This variable is called an *octal constant*, which I explain next.

Octal Constants

Octal constants are alternative ways to represent numeric constants. All leading zeros are ignored.

In Python 2, octal constants start with a 0 (zero):

```
oct_lit = 064
```

If we want to specify octal constants that execute in both Python 2 and 3, however, we must start with 0o (zero-oh):

```
oct_lit = 0o64
```

We can now change our octal constant line in the previous code snippet so that we run error-free code.

Using __future__

Let's change oct_lit = 064 to oct_lit = 0o64.

Download Numbers/future_withoct_torrentparser.py

```
from __future__ import division

def parse_torrent_id(arg):
    torrent_id = None
  oct_lit = 0o64
    if isinstance(arg, int):
        torrent_id = int(arg)
    elif isinstance(arg, float):
        torrent_id = int(arg)
        if torrent_id != arg:
            torrent_id = None
    else:
        try:
            torrent_id = int(arg)
            threshhold >= 6442450945
```

```
            if torrent_id >= threshhold / 2:
                torrent_id = None
            elif isinstance(torrent_id, float):
             torrent_id = threshhold // 2
        except (ValueError, TypeError):
            pass
        if torrent_id is None:
            try:
                int(arg, 16)
                torrent_id = arg
            except (ValueError, TypeError):
                pass
    return torrent_id, oct_lit
```

Using six

Again, let's change oct_lit = 064 to oct_lit = 0o64.

Download Numbers/six_withoctal_torrentparser.py
```
import six

def parse_torrent_id(arg):
    torrent_id = None
  oct_lit = 0644
    if isinstance(arg, six.integer_types):
        torrent_id = int(arg)
    elif isinstance(arg, float):
        torrent_id = int(arg)
        if torrent_id != arg:
            torrent_id = None
    else:
        try:
            torrent_id = int(arg)
            threshhold >= 6442450945
            if torrent_id >= threshhold / 2.0:
                torrent_id = None
            elif isinstance(torrent_id, float):
             torrent_id = threshhold // 2
        except (ValueError, TypeError):
            pass
        if torrent_id is None:
            try:
                int(arg, 16)
                torrent_id = arg
            except (ValueError, TypeError):
                pass
    return torrent_id, oct_lit
```

Summary

Integer inspection in Python 3 is done with checks against int because long is gone. For compatibility, use six's integer types constant or check against future's int type from the builtins module.

For float division, import division from the built-in __future__ package, and use Python 3 syntax to maintain compatibility.

TASK: ANOTHER PATCH

Today, your mentor Ali says that there is a script that looks like one from the open source project called Speed-control in the session.py source file under the transmissionrpc directory; except that this one only supports Python 2. Ali says that he needs your help with providing Python 3 support.

Download Numbers/session.py

```python
def _set_peer_port(self, port):
    """
    Set the peer port.
    """

    port2
    print (port2)
    if isinstance(port, long):
        self._fields['peer_port'] = Field(port, True)
        self._push()
    else:
        port = int(port) / 1
        self._fields['peer_port'] = Field(port, True)
        self._push()
```

Now let's see what was merged.

Using future

Download Numbers/future_session.py

```python
from __future__ import division

def _set_peer_port(self, port):
    """
    Set the peer port.
    """

    port2
    print (port2)
    if isinstance(port, int):
        self._fields['peer_port'] = Field(port, True)
        self._push()
    else:
        port = int(port) // 1
        self._fields['peer_port'] = Field(port, True)
        self._push()
```

Using six

Download Numbers/six_session.py

```
import six

def _set_peer_port(self, port):
        """
        Set the peer port.
        """
    port2
    print (port2)
    if isinstance(port, int):
        self._fields['peer_port'] = Field(port, True)
        self._push()
    else:
        port = int(port) // 1
        self._fields['peer_port'] = Field(port, True)
        self._push()
```

CHAPTER 3

Setting Metaclasses

Metaclasses are classes or objects that define a type/class of other classes. Metaclasses can be classes, functions, or any object that supports calling an interface. There are notable differences in setting a metaclass in Python 2 and 3. This chapter discusses the concepts for maintaining compatibility when setting metaclasses.

Metaclasses at a Glance

As in other languages, Python classes are blueprints from which we create objects; however, borrowing from languages like Smalltalk, Python classes are much more interesting. Classes are also first-class objects whose class is a metaclass. Simply put, metaclasses are classes of a class. With that said, since classes are objects, they can be used as parameters to functions: you can add attributes to them, you can copy them, and you can even assign them to variables. We can think of them this way:

```
SomeClass = MetaClass()
object = SomeClass()
```

In the background, Python uses the type function to create classes, since type is actually a metaclass. The type function is the metaclass that Python uses to create class objects, but you can also create your own metaclasses.

```
SomeClass = type('SomeClass', (), {})
```

Metaclasses are "class factories" used to create classes. Metaclasses give us a lot of power. They appear complicated but they are actually simple. They have many use cases; they help us intercept a class creation, modify a class, and return modified classes. Understanding how metaclasses work will earn you attention from your fellow Pythonistas.

Since metaclasses are powerful, you probably do not want to use them for extremely simple cases. There are other ways of altering a class, with methods like:

- Open Class (monkey patching)

- Using class decorators

Note Metaclasses are powerful, and with great power comes a lot of responsibility. If you are still wondering why you need metaclasses, then you probably are not supposed to be using them.

© Joannah Nanjekye 2017

J. Nanjekye, *Python 2 and 3 Compatibility*, https://doi.org/10.1007/978-1-4842-2955-2_3

There are other, cleaner ways to achieve your objectives in cases where you need custom metaclasses. Never use them just because you know how to; use them when you are certain.

Metaclasses are deeper magic than 99% of users should ever worry about. If you wonder whether you need them, you don't (the people who actually need them know with certainty that they need them, and don't need an explanation about why).

—Tim Peters, Python core developer

Metaclasses: The Python 2 Way

In Python 2, metaclasses are set by defining the __metaclass__ variable. This variable can be any callable accepting argument, such as name, bases, and dict. Let's create a class with a MyBase base class and a MyMeta metaclass.

Download Metaclasses/python2_metaclass.py

```python
class MyBase (object):
    pass

class MyMeta (type):
    pass

class MyClass (MyBase):
    __metaclass__ = MyMeta
    pass
```

We set the __metaclass__ variable to the custom metaclass.

Metaclasses in Python 3

In contrast, in Python 3, metaclasses are set using the keyword metaclass. We assign the custom metaclass to this keyword.

Download Metaclasses/python3_metaclass.py

```python
class MyBase (object):
    pass

class MyMeta (type):
    pass

class MyClass (MyBase, metaclass=MyMeta):
    pass
```

Metaclasses Compatibility

As discussed, there is contrast with how Python 2 and Python 3 handle metaclasses. The difference is in the syntax. Both Python-future and six offer wrappers to help us.

Using Python-future

Take a look at the following code. It is a Python 2 snippet that sets the MyMeta metaclass in the MyKlass class.

Download Metaclasses/example.py

```python
class MyMeta(type):
    def __new__(meta, name, bases, dct):
        print '-----------------------------------'
        print "Allocating memory for class", name
        print meta
        print bases
        print dct
        return super(MyMeta, meta).__new__(meta, name, bases, dct)
    def __init__(cls, name, bases, dct):
        print '-----------------------------------'
        print "Initializing class", name
        print cls
        print bases
        print dct
        super(MyMeta, cls).__init__(name, bases, dct)

class MyKlass(object):
    __metaclass__ = MyMeta
    def foo(self, param):
        pass
    barattr = 2
```

This metaclass makes some modifications to the MyKlass class when the class is created. More information on metaclasses is beyond the scope of this book, however. Our major concern here is where the metaclass is set, which is on the line with __metaclass__ = MyMeta. The concern is that Python 2 syntax will cause many errors when we run this code in Python 3, and yet we want to be in harmony with both Python versions.

To accommodate Python 2 and Python 3 using Python-future, we need to first import the with_metaclass module from future.utils. This module avails us with a with_metaclass method that takes two arguments. The first one is the metaclass that we want to set, and the second is the base class of our class. You can use an object if the class's ancestor is not specified.

■ **Note**   As always, the import of the with_metaclass module from future.utils should be at the very top of the module.

Changing this code gives us the following.

Download Metaclasses/future_metaclass_method.py

```python
from future.utils import with_metaclass
class MyMeta(type):
    def __new__(meta, name, bases, dct):
        print '-----------------------------------'
        print "Allocating memory for class", name
        print meta
        print bases
        print dct
        return super(MyMeta, meta).__new__(meta, name, bases, dct)
    def __init__(cls, name, bases, dct):
        print '-----------------------------------'
        print "Initializing class", name
        print cls
        print bases
        print dct
        super(MyMeta, cls).__init__(name, bases, dct)

class MyKlass(with_metaclass(MyMeta, object)):
    def foo(self, param):
        pass
    barattr = 2
```

As you can see, not much was done. We did our import of the with_metaclass module from the future. utils module. We then dropped the line that had the __metaclass__ = MyMeta definition. We instead introduced the with_metaclass() function in the class declaration. We gave this method two parameters. The first parameter is the name of the custom metaclass that you created (in this case, our custom metaclass is called MyMeta). The second parameter is the class ancestor, which is the object in this code.

Using six

six gives us two options for setting a metaclass on a class that will run reliably in both Python 2 and Python 3:

- the with_metaclass() method
- the add_metaclass() decorator

Using the with_metaclass() Method

The with_metaclass() method is required in the class declaration. It takes the metaclass and the base class as arguments, respectively. It is used like this:

Download Metaclasses/six_usage1.py

```python
from six import with_metaclass

class MyMeta(type):
    pass
```

```
class MyBase(object):
    pass

class MyClass(with_metaclass(MyMeta, MyBase)):
    pass
```

Apply this knowledge in the Python 2 code example using Python-future; the code changes as follows.

Download Metaclasses/six_metaclass_method.py

```
from six import with_metaclass

class MyMeta(type):
    def __new__(meta, name, bases, dct):
        print '----------------------------------'
        print "Allocating memory for class", name
        print meta
        print bases
        print dct
        return super(MyMeta, meta).__new__(meta, name, bases, dct)
    def __init__(cls, name, bases, dct):
        print '----------------------------------'
        print "Initializing class", name
        print cls
        print bases
        print dct
        super(MyMeta, cls).__init__(name, bases, dct)

class MyKlass(with_metaclass(MyMeta, object)):
    def foo(self, param):
        pass
    barattr = 2
```

The trick was importing the with_metaclass module from six and calling the `with_metaclass` method in the class declaration, with two parameters corresponding to the name of the custom metaclass (`MyMeta`). The second parameter is the class's super class (object).

Using the add_metaclass() Class Decorator

The `add_metaclass()` class decorator is applied on a class, which changes the class to one constructed with a metaclass; for example, the decorated class `Klass`.

Download Metaclasses/six_usage2.py

```
class MyMeta(type):
        pass

@add_metaclass(MyMeta)
class Klass(object):
        pass
```

becomes this in Python 3:

Download Metaclasses/six_usage2_output1.py

```
class myMeta(type):
        pass

class Klass(object, metaclass=MyMeta):
        pass
```

And it becomes this in Python 2:

Download Metaclasses/six_usage2_output2.py

```
class myMeta(type):
        pass

class Klass(object):
        __metaclass__ = MyMeta
        pass
```

■ **Note**   These class decorators require Python 2.6 and above.

If you want to emulate this class decorator behavior in Python 2.5, then you may have to do what's shown in the following code.

Download Metaclasses/six_usage2_py25.py

```
class MyMeta(type):
    pass

class MyKlass(object):
    pass

MyKlass = add_metaclass(MyMeta)(MyKlass)
```

Let's apply the six class decorator method to our previous Python 2 code example; the code changes to the following:

Download Metaclasses/six_decorator_method.py
```
import six

class MyMeta(type):
    def __new__(meta, name, bases, dct):
        print '---------------------------------'
        print "Allocating memory for class", name
        print meta
        print bases
        print dct
        return super(MyMeta, meta).__new__(meta, name, bases, dct)
```

```
    def __init__(cls, name, bases, dct):
        print '----------------------------------'
        print "Initializing class", name
        print cls
        print bases
        print dct
        super(MyMeta, cls).__init__(name, bases, dct)

@add_metaclass(MyMeta)
class MyKlass(object):
    def foo(self, param):
        pass
    barattr = 2
```

This is not rocket science. We just imported six; so no need for the with_metaclass module. Then we applied the @add_metaclass class decorator on our class. This decorator takes the name of the custom metaclass we want to set on the class.

■ **Note**   If you want to provide support for Python 2.5 in this example, then you may have to emulate this behavior using the workaround or trick discussed earlier in this section.

Summary

We discussed how to set metaclasses that will execute reliably in both Python 2 and Python 3 and just to reecho. Use the with_metaclass() function from either Python-future or six, and give it the right parameters. six also offers an add_metaclass decorator that we can use to maintain compatibility.

TASK: PREPARING A TUTORIAL ON METACLASSES

Today your mentor says that you should help him create a tutorial on metaclasses. The tutorial requires that you use code that executes correctly in both Python 2 and Python 3, because he anticipates the readers will use both versions (some may have not adopted Python 3 yet). He has a Python 2 script that he got from one of the online tutorials, which he wants you to convert so that it runs on both Python versions without errors. He says your solution should use both six and Python-future. Remember to open a pull request when you are done.

Download Metaclasses/task.py

```
class _TemplateMetaclass(type):

    pattern = r"""
%(delim)s(?:
  (?P<escaped>%(delim)s) |
  (?P<named>%(id)s)      |
```

```
        {(?P<braced>%(id)s)}   |
        (?P<invalid>)
    )
    """

    def __init__(cls, name, bases, dct):
        super(_TemplateMetaclass, cls).__init__(name, bases, dct)
        if 'pattern' in dct:
            pattern = cls.pattern
        else:
            pattern = _TemplateMetaclass.pattern % {
                'delim' : _re.escape(cls.delimiter),
                'id'    : cls.idpattern,
                }
        cls.pattern = _re.compile(pattern, _re.IGNORECASE | _re.VERBOSE)

class Template(object):
    __metaclass__ = _TemplateMetaclass

    delimiter = '$'
    idpattern = r'[_a-z][_a-z0-9]*'

    def __init__(self, template):
        self.template = template
```

Let's see if your solutions make it to what was merged.

Using Python-future

Download Metaclasses/future_task.py
```
from future.utils import with_metaclass

class _TemplateMetaclass(type):

    pattern = r"""
    %(delim)s(?:
      (?P<escaped>%(delim)s) |
      (?P<named>%(id)s)      |
      {(?P<braced>%(id)s)}   |
      (?P<invalid>)
    )
    """

    def __init__(cls, name, bases, dct):
        super(_TemplateMetaclass, cls).__init__(name, bases, dct)
        if 'pattern' in dct:
            pattern = cls.pattern
```

```
    else:
        pattern = _TemplateMetaclass.pattern % {
            'delim' : _re.escape(cls.delimiter),
            'id'    : cls.idpattern,
            }
    cls.pattern = _re.compile(pattern, _re.IGNORECASE | _re.VERBOSE)

class Template(with_metaclass(_TemplateMetaclass, object)):

    delimiter = '$'
    idpattern = r'[_a-z][_a-z0-9]*'

    def __init__(self, template):
        self.template = template
```

Using Six: The with_metaclass() Method

Download Metaclasses/six_with_metaclass_task.py

```python
from six import with_metaclass

class _TemplateMetaclass(type):

    pattern = r"""
    %(delim)s(?:
      (?P<escaped>%(delim)s) |
      (?P<named>%(id)s)      |
      {(?P<braced>%(id)s)}   |
      (?P<invalid>)
    )
    """

    def __init__(cls, name, bases, dct):
        super(_TemplateMetaclass, cls).__init__(name, bases, dct)
        if 'pattern' in dct:
            pattern = cls.pattern
        else:
            pattern = _TemplateMetaclass.pattern % {
                'delim' : _re.escape(cls.delimiter),
                'id'    : cls.idpattern,
                }
        cls.pattern = _re.compile(pattern, _re.IGNORECASE | _re.VERBOSE)

class Template(with_metaclass(_TemplateMetaclass, object)):

    delimiter = '$'
    idpattern = r'[_a-z][_a-z0-9]*'

    def __init__(self, template):
        self.template = template
```

The add_metaclass() Class Decorator

Download Metaclasses/six_with_classdecorator_task.py

```python
import six

class _TemplateMetaclass(type):

    pattern = r"""
    %(delim)s(?:
      (?P<escaped>%(delim)s)  |
      (?P<named>%(id)s)       |
      {(?P<braced>%(id)s)}    |
      (?P<invalid>)
    )
    """

    def __init__(cls, name, bases, dct):
        super(_TemplateMetaclass, cls).__init__(name, bases, dct)
        if 'pattern' in dct:
            pattern = cls.pattern
        else:
            pattern = _TemplateMetaclass.pattern % {
                'delim' : _re.escape(cls.delimiter),
                'id'    : cls.idpattern,
                }
        cls.pattern = _re.compile(pattern, _re.IGNORECASE | _re.VERBOSE)

@add_metaclass(_TemplateMetaclass)
class Template(object):

    delimiter = '$'
    idpattern = r'[_a-z][_a-z0-9]*'

    def __init__(self, template):
        self.template = template
```

CHAPTER 4

Strings and Bytes

Python 3 created a clear distinction between bytes and text, as opposed to Python 2 that uses the *str* type for both text and bytes. Python 2's idea of the *str* type led to a scenario where code worked for either type of data, or sometimes none. On the other hand, Python 3 requires that you care about when you are using text (as compared to binary data). This chapter describes how to absorb these differences in a single code base that can run in both Python versions. First, let's look at these differences.

Text and Binary Data

In Python 2, any string that appears in normal quotes are considered type *str*, which is used for representing both 8-bit Unicode (text) and binary data. There is also a *unicode* type for representing wide character text (Unicode text). The *unicode* type allows for an extra size of characters and more support for encoding and decoding.

On the other hand, Python 3 makes a very pronounced distinction between bytes and Unicode (text) strings. It comes with three string object types: *str*, *bytes*, and *bytearray*. The *str* type represents unicode text, which can be used by any programs which still need to process raw binary data that is not encoded per any text format for example Image files, and packed data. In contrast the *bytes* type represents binary data and is basically a sequence of small integers in the 0–255 range, which are printed as character strings instead of integers for convenience. The *bytearray* type is a mutable variant of the *bytes* type and supports the usual string operations that *str* and *bytes* do, but also has many of the same in-place change operations as lists.

This distinction of bytes and text in Python 3 means that the types are not interchangeable as opposed to Python 2 where these two types were seen as a single way of textual data input which therefore makes it easy to use either type interchangeably. With this distinction comes great responsibility of ensuring you use the right method when working with a given type. Table 4-1 lists *unique* methods for the *bytes* and *str* types.

Table 4-1. *Unique Methods*

str	bytes
encode()	decode()
isdecimal()	
isnumeric()	
format()	

© Joannah Nanjekye 2017
J. Nanjekye, *Python 2 and 3 Compatibility*, https://doi.org/10.1007/978-1-4842-2955-2_4

To handle these differences amicably, you should ensure that binary data is immediately decoded when received and if textual data needs to be sent as binary data then it has to be encoded as late as you can. This allows you to work with one data type, text and relieve you of any worries in keeping track of what data type you are working with in your code at any given point in time.

■ **Note** Python 3.5 introduced another __mod__ method to its bytes type. Therefore, formatting is supported for bytes.

These distinctions brought a couple of disruptions that introduced strings' and bytes' implementation incompatibilities. Let us look at how we can provide compatibility for these disruptions by first looking at unicode string literals.

As mentioned earlier, Python 3 enforces very loud and clear distinctions on bytes and text data compared to Python 2. The goal of compatibility is to ensure a common syntax for both versions despite these differences.

Unicode String Literals

We know that in a Python 2 code base, we mark string literals as unicode as

Download StringAndBytes/py2Unicode.py

```
string1 = 'The Aviation Alphabet'
string2 = u'aaaàçççñññ\n'
```

We either enclose the string in the normal quotes or we can decide to prefix the string with the *u* character. The following are a few ways to specify unicode string literals that are compatible in both Python 2 and 3:

- Explicit marking with a prefix

- Import unicode_literals from __future_

- Use six to classify the Unicode data

Explicit Marking with Prefix

It is advisable to explicitly mark a string literal with the *u leading* prefix (at the front of the string) to mark it as a Unicode string.

Download StringAndBytes/unicode_prefix.py

```
string1 = u'The Aviation Alphabet'
string2 = u'aaaàçççñññ\n'
```

This is useful when you need to upgrade an existing Python 2 code base to support Python 3. The futurize and Python-modernize tools don't do this for you automatically.

Import unicode_literals from __future_

We can also make use of the unicode_literals module from the __future__ builtin. This makes all string literals in the file or module to be unicode.

Download StringAndBytes/unicode_unicodeliterals.py

```
from __future__ import unicode_literals
string1 = 'Panpanpan'
string2 = 'Roger'
```

The import statement should appear at the very top of the module for effects to occur. This is useful if you are implementing a new code base or writing code for a completely new project.

six to Classify the Unicode Data

six provides a u() function that offers a Unicode string literal in both Python 2 and 3. The method takes text data that should be a normal string literal.

Download StringAndBytes/unicode_six.py

```
import six
string1 = six.u ('Panpanpan')
string2 = six.u ('Roger')
```

■ **Note**   In Python 3.3, the u prefix was introduced; therefore, If you need to support Python 3.3 and higher, there is no need for the u() method.

In summary, do the following to support both Python 2 and 3:

- Explicitly prefix the string literal with the *u* character when upgrading an existing Python 2 code base.

- Import the unicode_literals module from the __future__ builtin to make all string literals in the file or unicode module.

- Use the *u()* method from *six* to make unicode strings.

Byte String Literals

In the Python 2 code base, we can specify string literals as bytes as

Download StringAndBytes/py2Byte.py

```
string1 = 'The Aviation Alphabet'
```

We enclose the string in normal quotes.

There are two ways to specify byte string literals that are compatible in both Python 2 and 3:

- Explicit marking with a prefix
- Use six to classify the binary data

Explicit Marking with a Prefix

It is advisable to explicitly mark a string literal with the b *leading* prefix (at the front of the string) to mark it as a binary string.

Download StringAndBytes/byte_prefix.py

```
string1 = b'The Aviation Alphabet'
```

six to Classify the Binary Data

six provides a b() function that gives us a byte string literal in both Python 2 and Python 3. The method takes text data that should be a normal string literal.

Download StringAndBytes/byte_six.py

```
import six
string1 = six.b ('Panpanpan')
string2 = six.b ('Roger')
```

■ **Note**   Starting with Python 2.6, all versions support the b prefix; therefore, there is no need to use the b() method.

In summary, do the following to support both Python 2 and Python 3:

- Explicitly prefix the string literal with the b character.
- Use the b() method from six to make unicode strings.

This dichotomy of changes also effects how we access elements of strings, especially binary data.

Iterating Byte Strings

Accessing individual elements of binary data needs careful handling. While operations like slicing do not require special handling, the indexing into and looping of binary data needs more careful handling.

Indexing Binary Data

String objects are sequences of characters, while bytes or a bytearray are a sequence of integers in a range (0–255). representing a bytes or a bytearray object y. y[0] is an integer, while y[0:1] is a bytes or a bytearray object of length 1.

In Python 2, *bytes* and *str* are the same thing. This implies that indexing will return a one-item slice of bytes. This means that the following Python code:

```
b'123'[1]
```

returns:

```
b'2'
```

In Python 3, bytes are ideally a collection of binary numbers. Indexing returns the integer value for the byte that you index on. Therefore, this code:

```
b'123'[1]
```

returns:

```
50
```

Six to the Rescue

The six library provides an indexbytes() function that returns an integer, like in Python 3. We can use this function in our existing Python 2 code to return an integer as Python 3 intends.

Download StringAndBytes/bytes_indexing.py

```
import six

byte_string = b'123'
six.indexbytes(byte_string, 1).
```

This returns the byte at index position 1 in byte_string of the integer type, which is equivalent to the indexing binary data in Python 3.

Looping Binary Data

Python byte strings are just but a sequence of bytes. We often want to process these sequence of bytes each at a time using some of sort of looping technique. The cleaner, more readable, and faster way is using a for loop.

In Python 2, looping over byte strings takes this form:

Download StringAndBytes/bytes_loopingpy2.py

```
byte_string ='This is a byte-string.'
for bytechar in byte_string:
        do_stuff(bytechar)
```

This loops through the byte string obtaining one byte string. bytechar represents a one-item byte string of length 1 and not an integer.

In Python 3, looping over a byte string to access the one-item byte character shall involve an extra step of calling bytes() with the integer returned from the loop.

Download StringAndBytes/bytes_loopingpy3.py

```
byte_string = b'This is a byte-string.'
for someint in byte_string:
        bytechar = bytes(someint)
        do_stuff(bytechar)
```

The bytes() method explicitly converts the integer and the result is a one-item byte-string. This bytes() method is in the same format as encode(). It is cleaner than encode() because it does not require us to prefix b in front of quotes.

From these differences, we again see a need for a remedy for harmony so that looping binary data is seamless. We have two options to our rescue.

- Use the python-future's builtins module.

- Use the chr() and encode() methods.

Using Python-future's builtins Module

To have the same implementation of byte string looping, we shall import the bytes() method from future's builtins module.

Download StringAndBytes/bytes_loopingbuiltins.py

```
from builtins import bytes

byte_string = b'This is a byte-string.'
for someint in byte_string:
        bytechar = bytes(someint)
        do_stuff(bytechar)
```

This bytes() method works the same as the bytes() method in Python 3.

Using chr() and encode()

We can also convert the integer into a one character byte string using the ch() and encode(latin-1).

Download StringAndBytes/bytes_loopingch.py

```
from builtins import bytes, chr

byte_string = b'This is a byte-string.'
for someint in byte_string:
        char = chr(someint)
        bytechar = char.encode('latin-1')
        do_stuff(bytechar)
```

Six Byte Iteration

The six library has a six.iterbytes() function. This function will take a byte.

Download StringAndBytes/bytes_sixiteration.py

```
import six

byte_string = b'This is a byte-string.'
six.iterbytes(byte_string)
```

This method returns an iterator over bytes in byte_string as integers.
In summary,

- Use six.indexbytes() to perform bytearray indexing.

- Use chr() and encode() to loop through byte strings.

- You can also use bytes() method from the builtins module to convert the Python 3 returned integer to a one-item byte string.

- You can iterate bytes using six.iterbytes().

Base Strings

When we started off this chapter on strings, I mentioned that in Python 2 we had two types of string types *str* and *unicode*. These string types in Python 2 are in a hierarchy where they are descendants of a type basestring.

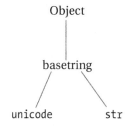

The type basestring in turn is a descendant of object. The basestring type is but a unification of the strings. We can use it to check whether an object is an instance of type *str* or *unicode*. Let's examine this code to appreciate its role in Python 2.

Download StringAndBytes/basestring.py

```
string1 = "echo"
string2 = u "lima"
isinstance    (string1, str)        #True
isinstance    (string2, str)        #False
isinstance(string1, unicode)        #False
isinstance(string2, unicode)        #True
isinstance(string1, basestring)     #True
isinstance(string2, basestring)     #True
```

Both strings are of type basestring but have their own types. When we perform an assertion on string2 being of type *str*, it returns False, and True for type *unicode*. When the same assertion is done for string1 on type *unicode*, the result is False, and True for type *str*.

Python 3 changed this hierarchy; instead, it has types *str* and *byte* as descendants of the base type object.

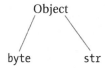

The tool 2to3 to replaces *basestring* with *str* because in Python 3 *str* represents Python 2's *str* and *unicode* types.

In Python 2, basestring exists solely for testing if a string is an instance of either type *str* or type *unicode*. It should not be called. Often, we have Python 2 code bases having code that is doing this testing:

Download StringAndBytes/basestring_py2.py

```
string1 = "echo"
string2 = u "lima"
isinstance(string1, basestring)     #True
isinstance(string2, basestring)     #True
```

We have already seen that Python 3 does not have this basestring type in its string hierarchy. To use Python 3 support for these checks, we have these alternatives:

- Use the basestring type from Python-future's past.builtins module.

- Check against the string_types constant from the six library.

- Check against *str* in the builtins module.

Python-future's past.builtins Module

Python-future has a past.builtins module that has a type basestring. This basestring type is the equivalent of *basestring* in Python 2 and *str* in Python 3.

Download StringAndBytes/basestring_future.py

```
from past.builtins import basestring

string1 = "echo"
string2 = u "lima"
isinstance(string1, basestring)     #True
isinstance(string2, basestring)     #True
```

six: string_types Constant

The constant *six*.string types represents all possible types of text data which is an equivalent of *basestring* in Python 2 and *str* in Python 3.

Download StringAndBytes/basestring_six.py

```
import six

string1 = "echo"
string2 = u "lima"
isinstance(string1, six.string_types)
isinstance(string2, six.string_bytes)
```

We import six and check against the string_types constants instead of basestring but as mentioned they are equivalent.

Check against str in the builtins Module

The very last alternative is to completely refactor the Python 2 code removing all considerations for byte-strings as strings. This means that we explicitly define strings of unicode with a u prefix, and bytes with a b prefix.

Download StringAndBytes/basestring_builtins.py

```
from builtins import str
string1 = u "echo"
string2 = u "lima"

string3 = b "echo"
string4 = b"lima"

res1 = string3 .decode()
res2 = string4 .decode()

assert isinstance(string1, str) and isinstance(res1, str)
assert isinstance(string2, str) and isinstance(res2, str)
```

We need to then decode all the bytes and check against the *str* type imported from the builtins module. This is the same as the Python 3 *str* module.

In summary, do the following to achieve compatibility:

- Check against the six.string_types.

- Check against the basestring type from Python-future's past.builtins module.

- Patiently refactor your Python 2 code to explicitly define strings of Unicode with a u prefix, and bytes with a b prefix, and check against the *str* type from the builtins module.

Now that we have explored how to work with all of these Python 2 string types, you must be wondering how StringIO works.

StringIO

StringIO generously gives us a file-like access to strings. We can use an existing module that deals with a file and make it work with strings without any changes. It gives us convenient ways of working with in memory text.

Typical use cases may be if you're building large strings, such as plain-text documents, and doing a lot of string concatenation, StringIO always does the magic rather than preforming a bunch of string concatenations. This is just one of the cases there are many cases where StringIO comes in very handy.

Python 2 has two implementations of StringIO, which are cStringIO and StringIO. The former was written in C for use if performance is important; while StringIO was written in Python for portability. Using these modules in Python 2 is this simple.

Download StringAndBytes/StringIO_py2.py

```
try:
    from cStringIO import StringIO
except:
    from io import StringIO

output = StringIO()
output.write('This goes into the buffer. ')

print output.getvalue()

output.close()

input = StringIO('Inital value for read buffer')

print input.read()
```

This code first imports the right StringIO implementation for the platform. We then write to the buffer, try to get what was written, discard the first buffer memory, initialize a read buffer, and finally, read from the buffer.

The sad news is these modules are long gone in Python 3 and we have to deal with this problem if we want our current Python 2 code to run seamlessly in Python 3. These modules all became the IO module. We have three ways of dealing with this problem:

- Use optional imports to import the required module on a given version.

- Use StringIO from the six module.

- Access StringIO from the six module from Python-future.

Optional Import of the Modules

We can use optional imports to import the required module on a given Python version. I have explained optional imports in the package imports chapter. Our Python 2 script now becomes:

Download StringAndBytes/StringIO_optionalimports.py

```
try:
    from StringIO import StringIO
except:
    from io import StringIO
```

```
output = StringIO()
output.write('This goes into the buffer. ')

print output.getvalue()

output.close()

input = StringIO('Inital value for read buffer')

print input.read()
```

This is how this works: when this script runs in Python 3, it tries to import the module in the try block, but this throws an exception because the module is gone. The right module in the except block is imported, and life goes on. In Python 2, execution is normal.

■ **Note** Working with import IO also works without errors in both Python 2 and Python 3.

StringIO from the six Module

six has a StringIO module that is an alias for StringIO.StringIO in Python 2, and for IO.StringIO in Python 3.

Download StringAndBytes/StringIO_six.py

```
import six

output = six.StringIO()
output.write('This goes into the buffer. ')

print output.getvalue()

output.close()

input = six.StringIO('Inital value for read buffer')

print input.read()
```

All we have to do is import six and use the StringIO method from the six module.

StringIO from the six Module from Python-future

This particular alternative is the most interesting as Python-future gives us a way of calling StringIO from six.

Download StringAndBytes/StringIO_future.py

```
from future.utils.six import StringIO
output = StringIO()
output.write('This goes into the buffer. ')
```

41

```
print output.getvalue()

output.close()

input = StringIO('Inital value for read buffer')

print input.read()
```

We are using StringIO from six through future.

BytesIO

Like StringIO, BytesIO is now in IO in Python 3 and no longer in StringIO, as in Python 2. We have the following two alternatives:

- Use BytesIO from the six module.
- Use BytesIO from the six module through Python-future.

BytesIO from the six Module

six has a BytesIO module that is an alias for StringIO.StringIO in Python 2, and for io.BytesIO in Python 3.

Download StringAndBytes/ByteIO_six.py

```
import six

output = six.BytesIO()
output.write('This goes into the buffer. ')

print output.getvalue()

output.close()

input = six.BytesIO('Inital value for read buffer')

print input.read()
```

All we have to do is import six and use the BytesIO method from the six module.

BytesIO from the six Module Through Python-future

Python-future provides a way to call BytesIO from six, which is interesting reuse instead of useless reengineering.

Download StringAndBytes/ByteIO_future.py

```
from future.utils.six import BytesIO

output = BytesIO()
output.write('This goes into the buffer. ')
```

```
print output.getvalue()

output.close()

input = ByteIO('Inital value for read buffer')

print input.read()
```

We are using BytesIO from six through future.
In summary,

- Use the BytesIO method from the six module.
- Use the same BytesIO in Python-future.

Summary

We looked at how to provide compatibility for strings. We discussed string aspects, such as basestrings, byte strings, text strings, and StringIO and ByteIO. The summaries at the end of every section act as good cheat sheets. Before we log out of this chapter, I have a task that you can look at to better appreciate the concepts in this chapter.

TASK: PFP-MASTER

Today, Ali, your mentor, dug up a very old method from the project pfp-master. It is located under the pfp directory in the fields.py source file. Ali says there is some ByteIO operations that he wants to port so that the script supports both Python 2 and 3. As always, prepare a commit with solutions using both Python-future and six, if possible. This script contains one method.

Download StringAndBytes/pfp-master_task.py

```python
from cStringIO import StringIO

def _pfp__pack_data(self):
        """Pack the nested field
        """
        if self._pfp__pack_type is None:
                return

        tmp_stream = BytesIO()
        self._._pfp__build(bitwrap.BitwrappedStream(tmp_stream))
        raw_data = tmp_stream.getvalue()

        unpack_func = self._pfp__packer
        unpack_args = []
        if self._pfp__packer is not None:
                npack_func = self._pfp__packer
                unpack_args = [true(), raw_data]
```

```
        elif self._pfp__pack is not None:
                unpack_func = self._pfp__pack
                unpack_args = [raw_data]

        # does not need to be converted to a char array
        If not isinstance(unpack_func, functions.NativeFunction):
                io_stream = bitwrap.BitwrappedStream(BytesIO(raw_data))
                unpack_args[-1] = Array(len(raw_data), Char, io_stream)

        res = unpack_func.call(unpack_args, *self._pfp__pack_func_call_info,
        no_cast=True)
        if isinstance(res, Array):
                res = res._pfp__build()

        io_stream = BytesIO(res)
        tmp_stream = bitwrap.BitwrappedStream(io_stream)

        self._pfp__no_unpack = True
        self._pfp__parse(tmp_stream)
        self._pfp__no_unpack = False
```

If you tried this, then you can check what was merged.

Using six

Let's import six and call the ByteIO method.

Download StringAndBytes/pfp-master_task_six.py

```
import six

def _pfp__pack_data(self):
        """Pack the nested field
        """
        if self._pfp__pack_type is None:
                return

        tmp_stream = six.BytesIO()
        self._._pfp__build(bitwrap.BitwrappedStream(tmp_stream))
        raw_data = tmp_stream.getvalue()

        unpack_func = self._pfp__packer
        unpack_args = []
        if self._pfp__packer is not None:
                npack_func = self._pfp__packer
                unpack_args = [true(), raw_data]
        elif self._pfp__pack is not None:
                unpack_func = self._pfp__pack
                unpack_args = [raw_data]
```

```
        # does not need to be converted to a char array
        If not isinstance(unpack_func, functions.NativeFunction):
                io_stream = bitwrap.BitwrappedStream(six.BytesIO(raw_data))
                unpack_args[-1] = Array(len(raw_data), Char, io_stream)

        res = unpack_func.call(unpack_args, *self._pfp__pack_func_call_info,
        no_cast=True)
        if isinstance(res, Array):
                res = res._pfp__build()

        io_stream = six.BytesIO(res)
        tmp_stream = bitwrap.BitwrappedStream(io_stream)

        self._pfp__no_unpack = True
        self._pfp__parse(tmp_stream)
        self._pfp__no_unpack = False
```

Using Python-future

Let's import and use ByteIO from future.utils.six.

Download StringAndBytes/pfp-master_task_future.py

```
from future.utils.six import ByteIO

def _pfp__pack_data(self):
        """Pack the nested field
        """
        if self._pfp__pack_type is None:
                return

        tmp_stream = BytesIO()
        self._._pfp__build(bitwrap.BitwrappedStream(tmp_stream))
        raw_data = tmp_stream.getvalue()

        unpack_func = self._pfp__packer
        unpack_args = []
        if self._pfp__packer is not None:
                npack_func = self._pfp__packer
                unpack_args = [true(), raw_data]
        elif self._pfp__pack is not None:
                unpack_func = self._pfp__pack
                unpack_args = [raw_data]

        # does not need to be converted to a char array
        If not isinstance(unpack_func, functions.NativeFunction):
                io_stream = bitwrap.BitwrappedStream(BytesIO(raw_data))
                unpack_args[-1] = Array(len(raw_data), Char, io_stream)
```

```
    res = unpack_func.call(unpack_args, *self._pfp__pack_func_call_info,
no_cast=True)
    if isinstance(res, Array):
            res = res._pfp__build()

    io_stream = BytesIO(res)
    tmp_stream = bitwrap.BitwrappedStream(io_stream)

    self._pfp__no_unpack = True
    self._pfp__parse(tmp_stream)
    self._pfp__no_unpack = False
```

## CHAPTER 5

Package Imports

Python 3 comes with syntax changes for imports within a package by requiring us to use the relative imports syntax. There are libraries with a different package import for each Python version; for example, the URL library urllib.request is for Python 3, and urllib2 is for Python 2. This chapter describes how to ensure compatibility with relative imports and how to import a suitable package based on the Python version.

Before I go in detail about compatibility with package imports, let me take you a step back and go through Python's importing infrastructure.

Python Imports

Like any other language when you start out, in Python, you always want to know how to import other modules or packages for logic or code reuse. Python has a very flexible importing infrastructure. We can perform package imports in the following ways:

- Regular imports
- Using from
- Local imports
- Optional imports
- Relative imports

Regular Imports

The regular import is most commonly used. It requires that you use the import keyword followed by the module or package that you want to import.

Download PackageImports/regular.py

```
import sys
import os, sys, time
import sys as system
import urllib.error
```

You can import one module or many modules or packages on the same line. It is also acceptable to rename a module as you chose by using the as keyword. Submodules importation is done using dot notation.

■ **Note**   Importing multiple modules on the same line is against the Python style guide. The recommended way is to import each package or module on a new line.

Using from

We use this kind of syntax when we want to import part or particular parts of a module or package, as opposed to the whole module or package.

Download PackageImports/usingfrom.py

```python
from os import path
from os import *
from os import path, walk
from os import (path, walk)
from os import path, \
                walk
```

Importing a particular module from a package is very succinct and gives readers of your code information about where the module was imported from.

We can also decide to import everything by using the *. This may clutter your name space, however. Take a case where you have defined a function or a top-level variable that has the same name as one of the imported modules. If you try to use the one from the os module, it will use the one that you defined instead. Therefore, it should be used sparingly with standard library modules like the Tkinter module.

You can also use *from* to import multiple items on the same line. If there are many items, it is recommended that you enclose them in parentheses. If the items continue to the next line, use Python's line continuation character, which is a backslash.

Local Imports

Performing imports at the top of the script places the imports in the global scope, where all methods in the file can access them. We can decide to put imports in a local scope, like in a method.

Download PackageImports/local.py

```python
import sys

def squareRoot(a):
    import math
    return math.sqrt(a)
```

The sys import is in the global scope, whereas the math import is in the local squareRoot method scope. When you define another method in the same script and try to use the math module, it results in an import error; however, the sys module can be used by any method in the script. Importing modules in a local scope is beneficial when the module to be imported is used by a function that is rarely called. In this case, you can import the module in the method's local scope.

Optional Imports

Optional imports are used when you have a preferred package or module that you want to use, but you want to specify a fall back in case the first module or package doesn't exist.

Download PackageImports/optional.py

```
try:
    from http.client import responses
except ImportError:
    try:
        from httplib import responses
    except ImportError:
        from BaseHTTPServer import BaseHTTPRequestHandler
```

The general idea is to try to import the desired module. If the module doesn't exist, then import the second module while catching the exception. Optional imports are used to support multiple versions of software or for speed-ups. I will discuss how to use optional parameters for neutral compatibility later in this chapter.

Relative Imports

In Python 2, when modules within a package need to reference each other, you use import foo or from foo import Bar. Python 3 and modern versions of Python 2 have syntax for relative path imports, as described in PEP 302, by using periods to determine how to relatively import other packages or modules. Suppose that we have a file structure akin to this:

```
RoboCop/
|
+--__init__.py
|
+--constants.py
|
+--robot.py
|
+--cop.py
```

Now suppose that robot.py needs to import the entire constants.py file and one class from cop.py. What needs to be done is described next.

Python 2

Let's use the from import syntax.

Download PackageImports/relative2.py

```
import constants
from cop import SomeCop
```

Python 3

When you need to import an entire module from elsewhere in your package, use the new from . import syntax. The period is actually a relative path from this file (robot.py) to the file that you want to import (constants.py).

Download PackageImports/relative2.py

```
from . import constants
from . cop import SomeCop
```

In this case, they are in the same directory, thus the single period. You can also import from the parent directory (from .. import another module) or a subdirectory.

We have looked at the different ways to perform package or module imports. Python 3 introduces new syntax for relative imports, some library developers have developed a different package, and some standard libraries have different names, based on the Python version.

We can provide compatibility in these situations by using optional imports for renamed modules or by changing the syntax for performing relative imports. Let me explain each of these options in detail.

Compatibility for Renamed Modules

There are modules that have been renamed across Python versions. One of these modules is the HTTP module. We use http.client to access the responses functionality in python 2, but we use httplib to access the responses functionality in python 3. To achieve compatibility in same code base, make use of optional imports.

Download PackageImports/optional.py

```
try:
    from http.client import responses
except ImportError:
        from httplib import responses
```

Let's use a try/except block to capture any errors if the first imported module does not exist. Then perform an import to the optional import in the except block. With renamed modules like the HTTP module, we import the Python 2 http.client package, which executes without errors in Python 2. When this snippet is run on Python 3, however, an exception is thrown, in which case we import the httplib module that Python 3 supports.

Optional imports offer ways to import optional dependencies. It tries to load the dependency in the try block, and if it is not present, it loads the dependency in the except block. This way, we can import renamed modules in Python 2 and 3.

Compatibility for Relative Imports

Let's suppose that we have the following imports relative to a package:

```
Package/
|
+--__init__.py
|
+--module1.py
|
+--rmodule2.py
|
+--module3.py
```

There are two alternatives to import module2 in module1. We can use the Python 3 syntax for relative imports, or import `absolute_import` from the built-in __future__ module.

Relative Path Import Syntax

Relative imports use a module's __name__ attribute to determine that module's position in the package hierarchy. If the module's name does not contain any package information, then relative imports are resolved as if the module were a top-level module, regardless of where the module is actually located on the file system.

```
from . import submodule2
```

This imports the submodule2 module relative to the current package. The dot indicates to step up a number of levels in the package hierarchy. In this case, we are stepping up one level in the hierarchy that is in the current package.

Using __future__

Python 3 has implicit relative imports turned off. To achieve this in Python 2, we can turn off implicit relative imports by using the absolute_import module in the __future__ built-in package.

```
from __future__ import absolute_import
```

Summary

In this chapter, we looked at how to achieve compatibility for modules that are renamed or have different names in Python 2 and Python 3. We also looked at how to provide compatibility for relative imports.

TASK: GECKO-DEV

You learned a lot about compatibility with package imports. Now, your mentor Ali says that there is a script from the gecko-dev project that he has meaning to work on, but has not had the time recently. He wants your help. The script performs ByteIO. Before he gives you links to the script, he wants you to know something about the following script.

Download PackageImports/task.py

```
from StringIO import StringIO

def test_BytesIO():
    fp = BytesIO()
    fp.write(b("hello"))
    assert fp.getvalue() == b("hello")
```

Ali says, "This script uses BytesIO from the Python 2 StringIO module. Without going into details, all I want you to do are the optional imports for the right modules for Python 2 and 3, respectively." He then says that the goal of your task is to import the StringIO.StringIO module for Python 2 and to import io.StringIO for Python 3. This is in the `test_six.py` source file script, in the `testing/web-platform/tests/tools/six` directory of the geck-dev project.

If you have committed, then you can now check what he merged.

Download PackageImports/solution.py

```
try:
    from StringIO import StringIO
except ImportError:
        from io import BytesIO

def test_BytesIO():
    fp = BytesIO()
    fp.write(b("hello"))
    assert fp.getvalue() == b("hello")
```

CHAPTER 6

Exceptions

Python provides a very concise way to handle exceptions, but Python 2 and 3 each have their own distinct syntax for exception handling. In Python 3, catching exception objects requires the as keyword; raising exceptions with arguments requires parentheses; and strings cannot be used as exceptions. This chapter describes how to achieve neutral compatibility for raising, catching exceptions, and exception chaining.

Raising Exceptions

Python allows us to raise exceptions in several ways using the raise statement. Other languages may use throw. We can specify three parameters when using the raise statement, namely, exception type, the exception argument, and traceback. Using the raise statement without any arguments re-raises the last exception. The general syntax for raising exceptions is:

```
raise [Exception [, args [, traceback]]]
```

The exception argument and traceback are optional. Let's examine how to raise exceptions in a way that is compatible with both Python 2 and 3. We will look at exceptions without a traceback first, and then exceptions with a traceback later.

Raising Exceptions Without a Traceback

Raising an exception without a traceback generally involves using the raise statement with only the exception name, like NameError, and an exception argument. Typical Python 2 syntax for this looks like this:

```
def func(value):
    raise ValueError, "funny value"
```

For this statement to execute reliably in both Python versions, it should be changed to this snippet:

```
def func(value):
    raise ValueError ("funny value")
```

We introduce parentheses around the exception argument.

© Joannah Nanjekye 2017
J. Nanjekye, *Python 2 and 3 Compatibility*, https://doi.org/10.1007/978-1-4842-2955-2_6

Raising Exceptions with a Traceback

Python also allows us to raise exceptions with a traceback. A traceback is a stack trace from the point of an exception handler, and down the call chain to the point where the exception was raised. The following is the Python 2 syntax for raising exceptions with a traceback:

```
def func(value):
    traceback = sys.exc_info()[2]
    raise ValueError, "funny value", traceback
```

The same method can be written in Python 3 with a small difference: parentheses around the exception argument and calling the with_traceback() method.

```
def func(value):
    traceback = sys.exc_info()[2]
    raise ValueError ("funny value").with_traceback(traceback)
```

For neutral compatibility, Python-future and six both offer wrappers for raising exceptions.

Using Python-future

We will import and use raise_ from the future.utils package to raise exceptions that run on both Python 2 and 3.

```
from future.utils import raise_

def func(value):
    traceback = sys.exc_info()[2]
    raise_ (ValueError, "funny value", traceback)
```

When we use raise_, we give it exception type, argument, and traceback as parameters.
Also, future offers the option to use the raise_with_traceback method from the future.utils package to achieve the same thing.

```
from future.utils import  raise_with_traceback

def func(value):
    raise_with_traceback(ValueError("dodgy value"))
```

Using six

Similarly, we can import and use raise_ from the six package to raise exceptions that run on both Python 2 and 3.

```
from six import raise_

def func(value):
    traceback = sys.exc_info()[2]
    raise_ (ValueError, "funny value", traceback)
```

When we use raise_, we give it exception type, argument, and traceback as parameters. In summary, when raising exceptions for compatibility

- exceptions without tracebacks introduce parentheses around the exception argument

- exceptions with tracebacks use raise_ from Python-future and six

Catching Exceptions

We need to have a catch-all except clause to catch exceptions in Python. try and except are Python keywords used to catch exceptions. The code within the try clause is executed statement by statement. If an exception occurs, the rest of the try block is skipped, and the except clause is executed.

This is a simple way to catch exceptions in Python 2:

```
(x,y) = (5,0)

try:
        z = x/y
except ZeroDivisionError, e:
        print e
```

An except clause may name multiple exceptions as a parenthesized tuple; for example, (ZerDivionError, IdontLikeYouException). before the comma separating the exception and the *e* variable.

Separating the exception from the variable with a comma works in Python 2, but it has been deprecated and it does not work in Python 3. Use the as keyword instead of a comma for neutral compatibility. This is the default syntax in Python 3, but it works in both python versions.

```
(x,y) = (5,0)
try:
    z = x/y
except ZeroDivisionError as e:
    z = e
    print z
```

The as keyword assigns the exception to a variable, such as *e* in our case, which is also the most common, but you may give this variable a different name. The variable is an Exception instance.

In summary, use the as keyword (instead of a comma) for compatibility in catching exceptions.

Exception Chaining

Exception chaining rethrows a caught exception after wrapping it inside a new exception. The original exception is saved as a property of the new exception. Exception chaining is implicit if one exception causes another. This means that the first exception's information is available in the stack trace because it is stored in the __context__ attribute of the last exception class. Exception chaining may also be explicit if we associate a new exception when an exception is raised. This is used to translate one exception type to another. The original exception type is stored in the __cause__ attribute.

Exception chaining is only available in Python 3, in which we can write the following:

Download PackageImports/exceptionchaining_Python3.py

```
try:
    v = {}['a']
except KeyError as e:
    raise ValueError('failed') from e
```

There is no direct way to achieve exception chaining in Python 2, but we may do the same thing by adding custom attributes to our exception class, as follows:

Download PackageImports/exceptionchaining_Python2.py

```
class MyError(Exception):
    def __init__(self, message, cause):
        super(MyError, self).__init__(message + u', caused by ' + repr(cause))
        self.cause = cause

try:
    v = {}['a']
except KeyError as e:
    raise MyError('failed', e)
```

We add custom attributes to our MyError class. For a neutral code base, Python-future and six both provide a raise_from wrapper to handle exception chaining.

Using Python-future

We will import and use the raise_from module from the future.utils package.

Download PackageImports/exceptionchaining_future.py

```
from future.utils import raise_from

try:
    v = {}['a']
except KeyError as e:
    raise_from (MyError('failed', e))
```

The raise_from wrapper replaces the raise keyword.

Using Six

We will import and use the raise_from module from the six package.

Download PackageImports/exceptionchaining_six.py

```
from six import raise_from
```

```
try:
    v = {}['a']
except KeyError as e:
    raise_from (MyError('failed', e))
```

The raise_from wrapper replaces the raise keyword.

In summary, use Python-future's and six's raise_from wrapper for compatibility in exception chaining.

Summary

We looked at how to support Python 3 in a Python 2 code base for raising and catching exceptions, and with exception chaining.

TASK: RANDOM METHOD FROM ALI

Today Ali shot you an email on a Python 2 script that he wants you to work on to get it compatible with Python 3.

Download PackageImports/task.py

```
def foo(i):
    l = [1,2,3]
    try:
        assert i >= 1
        return l[i]
    except TypeError,e:
        print "dealing with TypeError"
    except IndexError, e:
        print "dealing with IndexError"
    except:
        print "oh dear"
    finally:
        print "the end"
```

He claims that the only problem with this script is the way that exceptions have been implemented. They still use Python 2 syntax, which does not work in Python 3.

The following was merged.

Download PackageImports/solution.py

```
def foo(i):
    l = [1,2,3]
    try:
        assert i >= 1
        return l[i]
    except TypeError as e:
        print "dealing with TypeError"
```

```
        except IndexError as e:
            print "dealing with IndexError"
        except:
            print "oh dear"
        finally:
            print "the end"
```

The syntax was changed to use as instead of the deprecated Python 2 comma.

## CHAPTER 7

HTML Processing

Python has always been shipped with a cgi module to escape different characters, but this has limitations. Starting with Python 3.2, the HTML module curbs these shortcomings. HTML parsing and entities are achieved using different modules in Python 2 and 3, which makes compatibility even harder to achieve. This chapter describes ways of implementing HTML escaping, and parsing that work in both Python 2 and 3.

HTML Escaping

Python has always been shipped with a cgi module with an escape() function to escape different characters in versions prior to 3.2. For example, the following script escapes < to &lt, > to &gt and & to &amp.

Download HTMLProcessing/cgi_escapepy

```
import cgi
s = cgi.escape( """& < >""" )
```

This script uses the cgi.escape()method to escape the &, >, and < characters. It converts these special characters into valid HTML tags. If it is used with the optional quote argument, as shown in the following, it also escapes the ".

```
cgi.escape(string_to_escape, quote=True)
```

The optional second parameter on cgi.escape escapes quotes. By default, they are not escaped. The cgi.escape() method has a limitation: it will not escape any characters other than &, >, and <; for example, apostrophes. This led to the introduction of the html module in Python 3.2+.

The html Module

The html module was introduced in Python 3.2 to escape reserved characters from HTML markup. Like the cgi module, it also has an escape() method.

Download HTMLProcessing/html_escape.py

```
import html

html.escape( """& < ' " >""" )
```

html.escape() differs from cgi.escape() in its defaults to quote=True.

Therefore, there are two different ways to achieve HTML escaping in the two Python versions, but we need to find a unified way of doing the same. Python-future can come to our rescue.

Using Python-future

Python-future provides the escape() method wrapper from its html module to help us get around the version differences:

Download HTMLProcessing/html_future.py

```
from html import escape

html.escape( """& < ' " >""" )
```

HTML Parsing

According to Wikipedia, parsing or syntactic analysis, is the process of analyzing a string of symbols, either in natural language or in computer languages, according to the rules of a formal grammar. The term *parsing* comes from Latin pars.

HTML parsing takes HTML code and extracts all relevant information from it, including paragraphs, dates, bold text, and so on.

In Python 2, HTML parsing is implemented as:

Download HTMLProcessing/html_parsingf_py2.py

```
from HTMLParser import HTMLParser

class MyHTMLParser(HTMLParser):
    def handle_starttag(self, tag, attrs):
        print("Encountered a start tag:", tag)

    def handle_endtag(self, tag):
        print("Encountered an end tag :", tag)

    def handle_data(self, data):
        print("Encountered some data  :", data)
```

In Python 3, however, the module changed from HTMLParser to html.parser.

Download HTMLProcessing/html_parsingf_py2.py

```
from HTMLParser import HTMLParser

class MyHTMLParser(HTMLParser):

    def handle_starttag(self, tag, attrs):
        print("Encountered a start tag:", tag)

    def handle_endtag(self, tag):
        print("Encountered an end tag :", tag)
```

```
def handle_data(self, data):
    print("Encountered some data  :", data)
```

Therefore, there are two different ways to achieve HTML parsing in the two Python versions, but we need to find a unified way of doing the same. We have three alternatives:

- Use the html.parser from Python-future
- Use the future.moves.html.parser from Python-future
- Use html_parser from six.moves

Using Python-future

Python-future offers two alternatives: the html.parser module and the future.moves.html.parser.

Using HTMLParser from html.parser

Let's import the relevant HTMLParser from the html.parser module. It allows us to achieve the intended compatibility.

Download HTMLProcessing/html_escape_future1.py

```python
from html.parser import HTMLParser

class MyHTMLParser(HTMLParser):
    def handle_starttag(self, tag, attrs):
        print("Encountered a start tag:", tag)

    def handle_endtag(self, tag):
        print("Encountered an end tag :", tag)

    def handle_data(self, data):
        print("Encountered some data  :", data)
```

Using HTMLParser from future.moves.html.parser

As in the first option, we will import HTMLParser from the future.moves.html.parser module. This will give us the intended compatibility.

Download HTMLProcessing/html_escape_future2.py

```python
from future.moves.html.parser  import HTMLParser

class MyHTMLParser(HTMLParser):
    def handle_starttag(self, tag, attrs):
        print("Encountered a start tag:", tag)
```

```
def handle_endtag(self, tag):
    print("Encountered an end tag :", tag)

def handle_data(self, data):
    print("Encountered some data  :", data)
```

Using six

six provides a consistent interface to load the module for parsing HTML on Python 2 or Python 3.

Download HTMLProcessing/html_escape_six.py

```
from six.moves import HTMLParser

class MyHTMLParser(HTMLParser):
    def handle_starttag(self, tag, attrs):
        print("Encountered a start tag:", tag)

    def handle_endtag(self, tag):
        print("Encountered an end tag :", tag)

    def handle_data(self, data):
        print("Encountered some data  :", data)
```

Summary

We looked at how to achieve compatibility when escaping and parsing HTML. Next, we will discuss the compatibility of files.

TASK: HTML PARSING

The following is a Python 2 script that does some HTML parsing. Your mentor is on stand-by to help you if you need clarity.

Download HTMLProcessing/task.py

```
class MyHTMLParser(HTMLParser):
    def handle_starttag(self, tag, attrs):
        print "Encountered a start tag:", tag
    def handle_endtag(self, tag):
        print "Encountered an end tag :", tag
    def handle_data(self, data):
        print "Encountered some data  :", data
```

Using six

This should be

Download HTMLProcessing/task_six.py

```
From six.moves import HTMLParser
class MyHTMLParser(HTMLParser):
    def handle_starttag(self, tag, attrs):
        print "Encountered a start tag:", tag
    def handle_endtag(self, tag):
        print "Encountered an end tag :", tag
    def handle_data(self, data):
        print "Encountered some data  :", data
```

CHAPTER 8

Working with Files

Every operating system makes use of files as the primary storage mechanism, and as such, there are mechanisms that allow us open and read from these files. Python also provides methods for opening, reading, and writing from files, but there are significant differences regarding how Python 2 and 3 handles file processing. This chapter explains the differences and shows neutral ways of performing file processing for compatibility on both versions using the io.open method.

File Processing

Before we look at compatibility in files, I will chitchat a bit about general file processing. Before we can do anything to a file, we have to open the file. In both versions 2 and 3, Python has a built-in open() function, which takes a file name as an argument. It takes a second argument in Python 3, the encoding argument. It doesn't take an encoding argument in Python 2.

File processing in Python 2 takes this form:

Download Files/open.py

```
f = open('some_file.txt')
data = f.read()
text = data.decode('utf-8')
```

This script opens a file and reads it. The data variable contains the read content, which are byte strings. We know that a file on a disk contains a sequence of bytes. In most cases, we are not interested in a sequence of bytes but instead want a sequence of Unicode characters (string).

To convert the byte sequence to a sequence of Unicode characters that is a string, Python has to decode the bytes according to a specific encoding algorithm.

In Python 3, if we do not specify character encoding, the default encoding shall be used, which may not support the characters in the file. In Python 3, opening a file without specifying encoding does this:

```
>>> file = open("email.docx")
>>> strw = file.read()
Traceback (most recent call last):
  File "<stdin>", line 1, in <module>
  File "/usr/lib/Python3.5/codecs.py", line 321, in decode
    (result, consumed) = self._buffer_decode(data, self.errors, final)
UnicodeDecodeError: 'utf-8' codec can't decode byte 0xb7 in position 10: invalid start byte
>>>
```

© Joannah Nanjekye 2017
J. Nanjekye, *Python 2 and 3 Compatibility*, https://doi.org/10.1007/978-1-4842-2955-2_8

First and foremost, default encoding is platform dependent. The preceding code may work on someone else's computer if their default character encoding is UTF-8, but it will fail on another person's computer if their default character encoding is not UTF-8.

The remedy is to use methods that allow us to specify character encoding that does not resort to using the default encoding, which is very inconsistent and doesn't bring harmony to our programs as default character encoding is platform dependent.

There are two ways to do this: one is by using io.open() and the second is using codecs.open(). Both methods take a second argument, which is the character encoding, but Python 3 rendered codecs.open() obsolete, which leaves us with the one option of using io.open() since it works in both Python 2 and 3.

If you are curious, I will show how we can specify character encoding using codecs.open() in Python 2.

Download Files/codecs.py

```
import codecs
f = codecs.open('some_file.txt', encoding="utf-8")
```

■ **Note**   codecs.open() is deprecated and obsolete in Python 3; use io.open() or the built-in open().

---

io.open()

This method is supported in both Python 2 and 3 and it also allows us to specify character encoding.

To support Python 2.6 and later versions, including Python 3.4, use io.open(), which takes an encoding argument instead of codecs.open(), which is now obsolete.

To write compatible code for file processing, we have two ways to achieve this:

- Specify encoding on opening the file

- Open the file, read the bytes, and decode them with a specific encoding

Specifying Encoding on Opening the File

We can specify the mode as second parameter on the open function, and in this case, the read data won't have to be decoded using a given encoding.

Download Files/ioOpening.py

```
from io import open

f = open('myfile.txt', encoding='utf-8')
text = f.read()
```

We are using the open() method from the io module and not the built-in open() method. The method will take first the file name, which is a relative path but also goes on to take the encoding argument. You can use any encoding argument depending on the data in the file. I simply chose UTF-8 for this example.

There is no need to decode this data again; after specifying a decoding argument on opening, whatever is read is Unicode text.

We may decide to open the file and specify that we will read Unicode text using the *rt* keyword instead of using the encoding argument. It works the same way.

Download Files/ioDecodert.py

```
from io import open

f = open('some_file.txt', 'rt')
data = f.read()
```

Whatever is read in this case is Unicode text; no need for a decoding step. You can also open and read bytes:

Download Files/ioDecodert.py

```
from io import open

f = open('some_file.txt', 'rb)
```

Specifying Encoding on Decode

We can specify the encoding argument as a parameter on the decode function when decoding the read data.

Download Files/ioDecoderb.py

```
from io import open

f = open('some_file.txt', 'rb')
data = f.read()
text = data.decode('utf-8')
```

We are using the open() method from the io module and not the built-in open() method. The first argument is the filename, which is a relative path. The second argument specifies that we should read bytes using rb. This is how we read binary files: by using the open() function with rb or wb mode to read or write binary data. Therefore, when we read the contents of the file, they are bytes and should be decoded using a specific encoding algorithm.

Python 3 open() builtin

You must be wondering what became of the open() builtin in Python 3. It became an alias to io.open() and works the same way io.open() works. This implies that it also takes a second encoding argument. Therefore using the open() builtin in Python 3 takes this form :

Download Files/opnepy3.py

```
f = open('myfile.txt', encoding='utf-8')
text = f.read()
```

It is used in the very same way io.open() is used.

Summary

We have looked at how to work with files in a way that is compatible with both Python 2 and 3.

TASK: HELP A STACK OVERFLOW USER

Today, someone on Stack Overflow asked a question and provided the following Python 2 function while seeking help. Your mentor says that you could be of help to this person. Study this code and reimplement it to be compatible.

Download Files/task.py

```python
def read_text():
    quotes = open("C:\Python27\houston.txt")
    Contents = quotes.read()
    quotes.close()
```

"Your final answer to this user should look similar to this solution," says Ali.

Download Files/task.py

```python
def read_text():
    quotes = open("C:\Python27\houston.txt", "r")
    Contents = quotes.read()
    quotes.close()
```

■ ■ ■

## CHAPTER 9

Custom Behavior of Classes

In Python, class method names that start and end with __ are referred to as *special methods* because they allow us to customize the way Python will use our classes. In this chapter, we look at some of these methods and learn how to achieve compatibility in both Python 2 and 3. We first look at the custom iterator methods (__iter__ and __next__) and then later discuss the __str__, and __nonzero__ methods.

Custom Iterators

Iterators in Python and other languages are objects that can be iterated. Iterators are all over Python. They have been subconsciously implemented in for loops, comprehensions, and generators, to mention but a few. An iterable object supports creating iterators over its contents. Most built-ins and containers in Python—such as list, tuple, and string—are iterables.

In Python, for an object to be called an *iterator*, it must implement the __iter__ and __next__ special methods, collectively referred to as the *iterator protocol*. This implies that we can build our own custom iterators using the __iter__() and __next__() special methods. The __iter__() method returns the iterator object its self and the __next__() method returns the next value from the iterator. If there are no more items to return, then it will raise the StopIteration exception. Iterator objects can only be used once because after a StopIteration exception has been raised, it will keep raising this same exception.

Most special methods should never be called directly; instead, we use a for loop or list comprehension, and then Python will call the methods automatically. If you need to call them, use Python's built-ins: iter and next.

■ **Note** By definition, an iterable—is an object that has the __iter__ method defined and an iterator—is an object that has both __iter__ and __next__ defined, where __iter__ returns the iterator object and __next__ returns the next element in the iteration.

After creating an iterator class, we can then create an iterator and iterate through it using the next() function or most conveniently, we can use the for loop. It is not a rule of thumb that an iterator object must exhaust or rather have an end. Iterator objects can be infinite but with great care taken to handle such iterators.

© Joannah Nanjekye 2017

J. Nanjekye, *Python 2 and 3 Compatibility*, https://doi.org/10.1007/978-1-4842-2955-2_9

In Python 2, the rules for creating iterator classes still hold (iterator protocol), but unlike Python 3, it uses next() instead of the __next__ special method.

Download CustomBehaviourOfClasses/Python2_CustomIterator.py

```python
class PgCounter(object):
    def __init__(self, min, max):
        self.current = min
        self.max = max

    def __iter__(self):
        return self

    def next (self):
        if self.current > self.max:
            raise StopIteration
        else:
            self.current += 1
            return self.current - 1
```

The Class implements an __iter__() method, which returns itself as an iterator object. It also implements the next() method, which returns the next value until current is lower that max. This is a whole iterator class abiding by the iterator protocol.

We can now use this iterator in our code.

Download CustomBehaviourOfClasses/Python2_CustomIteratorUse.py

```python
itr = PgCounter('hello')
assert itr.next() == 'H'
assert list(itr) == list('ELLO')
```

To make the preceding Python class and its method logic neutral-compatible, we have three alternatives.

- Subclass object from the future's builtins module
- Use the @implements_iterator decorator from future
- Subclass Iterator and use the advance_iterator() method from six

Subclass Object from future's builtins Module

We earlier saw that to create custom iterators, we must implement __iter__ and __next__. We also know that in Python 2, __next__ is next(). The object subclass used in Python 2 allows next() but still provides the next -> __next__ alias.

Download CustomBehaviourOfClasses/CustomIterator_builtins.py

```python
from builtins import object

class PgCounter(object):
    def __init__(self, min, max):
        self.current = min
        self.max = max
```

```python
    def __iter__(self):
        return self

    def __next__ (self):
        if self.current > self.max:
            raise StopIteration
        else:
            self.current += 1
            return self.current - 1

    __metaclass__ = MyMeta
    pass
```

When given the next -> __next__ alias, we can use the Python 3 syntax (__next__) and have compatibility in both versions for the iterator interface. The iterator can also now be used in our code the Python 3 way.

Download CustomBehaviourOfClasses/CustomIteratorUse_builtins.py

```python
itr = PgCounter('hello')
assert next() == 'H'
assert list(itr) == list('ELLO')
```

We are now using the Python 3 syntax next() instead of itr.next().
In summary,

1. Import the object class from the future's builtins module.

2. The object class from the future's builtins module gives us the next -> __next__ alias functionality.

3. Use Python 3 syntax for the iterator interface (__next__) and use the Python 3 style (next()) to get the next value in the iterator.

The @implements_iterator Decorator from future

future allows the Python 3 syntax for the iterator interface (next) to get the next value in the iterator.

Download CustomBehaviourOfClasses/CustomIterator_future.py

```python
from future.utils import implements_iterator

@implements_iterator
class PgCounter(object):
    def __init__(self, min, max):
        self.current = min
        self.max = max

    def __iter__(self):
        return self
```

```
def __next__ (self):
    if self.current > self.max:
        raise StopIteration
    else:
        self.current += 1
        return self.current - 1
```

Import the decorator from the future.utils module and decorate the iterator class as before. Get the next value in the iterable.

Download CustomBehaviourOfClasses/CustomIteratorUse_future.py

```
itr = PgCounter('hello')
assert next() == 'H'
assert list(itr) == list('ELLO')
```

We are still using the Python 3 syntax next() instead of itr.next().
In summary,

1. Import the @implements_iterator from future.utils.

2. Decorate the iterator class.

3. And use Python 3 syntax for the iterator interface and getting the next item in the iterator.

Iterator Class and Advanced_iterator() from six

Six provides an Iterator class that helps us create portable iterators. This class should be subclassed, and the subclasses should implement a __next__ method.

Download CustomBehaviourOfClasses/CustomIterator_six.py

```
import six

class PgCounter(six.Iterator):
    def __init__(self, min, max):
        self.current = min
        self.max = max

    def __iter__(self):
        return self

    def __next__ (self):
        if self.current > self.max:
            raise StopIteration
        else:
            self.current += 1
            return self.current - 1
```

This Iterator class has only one method in Python 2. It is empty in Python 3; it is just aliased to the object.

To get the next item in the iterator, we use the advanced_iterator() method to achieve our compatibility goals.

Download CustomBehaviourOfClasses/CustomIteratorUse_six.py

```
itr = PgCounter('hello')
assert six.advance_iterator (itr) == 'H'
assert list(itr) == list('ELLO')
```

The six.advanced_iterator() method returns the next item in our iterator. This replaces the need for us to call itr.next() in Python 2 and next(itr) in Python 3.

In summary,

1. Import six.

2. Subclass the iterator class with six.Iterator.

3. Use the six.advanced_iterator() method instead of next() in Python 3 and itr.next() in Python 2.

4. The six.advanced_iterator() method takes the iterator instance as an argument.

■ **Note**   It is advisable that all code uses the builtin next().

Exercise 7.1

Make the following script compatible.

Download CustomBehaviourOfClasses/CustomIterator_Exercise.py

```
def test_iterator():
    class myiter(object):
        def next(self):
            return 13
    assert myiter().next()== 13
    class myitersub(myiter):
        def next(self):
            return 14
    assert myitersub().next() == 14
```

Custom __str__ Methods

__str__ is a special method like __init__, __next__, and __iter__. It is used to return a string representation of an object.

Here is an example:

Download CustomBehaviourOfClasses/str_example.py

```
Class MyDate:
    def __str__(self):
        return "The date today"
```

This is the str method for the MyDate objects. When we print an object of this class, Python invokes or calls the str method.

```
>>> date = MyDate()
>>> print date
The date today
```

The __str__ method has a closely related method, __repr__, which also returns a string representation of an object but with subtle differences. Take the following code for example.

```
>>> num = 4
>>> repr (num)
'4'
>>> str(4)
'4'
>>> name = "jason"
>>> repr (name)
"'jason'"
>>> str (name)
'jason'
>>> name2 = eval(repr(name))
>>> name3 = eval(str(name))
Traceback (most recent call last):
  File "<stdin>", line 1, in <module>
  File "<string>", line 1, in <module>
NameError: name 'jason' is not defined
```

The results of repr() and str() are the same for integers, but when it comes to strings, then we begin to see a difference. The biggest difference is when we try to use the results of the methods as arguments to eval(). A repr() implementation for a str object can be used as an argument to *eval()*, returning a valid str object. An str() implementation does not return a valid value.

According to the official Python documentation, __repr__ is referred to as the official object representation, whereas __str__ is the formal representation. It is argued that an official representational should be callable by eval() and must return the same object.

__str__ is also better in some cases because __str__ representations of objects are more readable than __repr__ representations.

```
>>> from datetime import datetime
>>> now = datetime.now()
>>> repr(now)
'datetime.datetime(2017, 8, 10, 17, 23, 34, 64394)'
>>> str(now)
'2017-08-10 17:23:34.064394'
>>>
```

The output given by __repr__() is very useful for debugging in development, while the output of __str__ may be useful to the user of the application.

■ **Note** The __str__ and __repr__ methods are used in the builtin str() and repr() methods, respectively.

Exercise 7.2

Print the string representations of the following classes.

Download CustomBehaviourOfClasses/str_exercise.py

```
class cartesian:
    def __init__(self, x=0, y=0):
        self.x, self.y = x, y
    def distanceToOrigin(self):
        return floor(sqrt(self.x**2 + self.y**2))
  class manhattan:
    def __init__(self, x=0, y=0):
        self.x, self.y = x, y
    def distanceToOrigin(self):
        return self.x + self.y
```

In Python 2, the __str__ method returns bytes. If we want to return characters, then we have to implement another __unicode__() method that returns characters.

Download CustomBehaviourOfClasses/str_py2.py

```
class Name():
    def __unicode__(self):
        return 'character string: \u5b54\u5b50'
    def __str__(self):
        return unicode(self).encode('utf-8')

a = MyClass()
print(a)
```

We should put all string formatting in the __unicode__() method, and then create the __str__() method as a stub that calls unicode().

In Python 3, __str__ () returns character strings. There is a relevant __bytes__ special method that returns bytes.

Download CustomBehaviourOfClasses/str_py3.py

```
class Name():
    def __str__(self):
        return u "Je nun"

a = MyClass()
print(a)
```

The print statement returns a character string.

Exercise 7.3

Print the byte string representations of the following code.

Download CustomBehaviourOfClasses/byte_exercise.py

```
class Name():
    def __str__(self):
        return u "Je nun"

a = MyClass()
print(a)
```

Python 2 code implements the __str__ method, as illustrated. To support Python 3, we can use either the @Python_2_unicode_compatible decorator availed by the future library or the @six.Python_2_unicode_compatible six decorator. Let's get to the details about each of these decorators.

future: @Python_2_unicode_compatible Decorator

The @Python_2_unicode_compatible decorator takes the method class that implements the __str__ method.

Download CustomBehaviourOfClasses/str_future.py

```
from future.utils import Python_2_unicode_compatible

@Python_2_unicode_compatible
class SomeClass(object):
    def __str__(self):
        return u' some unicode : \u5b54\u5b50'

res = SomeClass()
print(res)
```

In Python 3, the decorator does nothing, but in Python 2, it will alias __str__ with __unicode__.
In summary,

1. Import Python_2_unicode_compatible from future.utils.

2. Decorate the class with @Python_2_unicode_compatible.

3. Use Python 3 syntax.

Exercise 7.4

Make the following Python 2 script compatible with both Python 2 and Python 3 using future. The hello string should be printed as a character string, and then as a byte string. Hint: the solution should implement __byte__ and __str__.

Download CustomBehaviourOfClasses/str_future_exercise.py

```python
def test_Python_2_unicode_compatible():
    class MyTest(object):
        def __unicode__(self):
                return 'hello'
                def __str__(self):
            return unicode(self).encode('utf-8')


            def __str__(self):
            return 'hello'

    my_test = MyTest()
```

six: @Python_2_unicode_compatible Decorator

Similar to future, six has a @Python_2_unicode_compatible decorator takes the method class that implements the __str__ method.

Download CustomBehaviourOfClasses/str_six.py

```python
import six

six.@Python_2_unicode_compatible
class SomeClass(object):
    def __str__(self):
        return u' some unicode : \u5b54\u5b50'

res = SomeClass()
print(res)
```

The decorator does nothing in Python 3 but will alias __str__ to __unicode__ and create a __str__ method that returns the result of unicode(), which is a string encoded with UTF-8.

In summary,

1. Import six.

2. Decorate the class with @Python_2_unicode_compatible.

3. Use Python 3 syntax.

Exercise 7.5

Make the following Python 2 script compatible to both Python 2 and Python 3 using six.

Download CustomBehaviourOfClasses/str_six_exercise.py

```python
class TestClass(object):
    def __unicode__(self):
                    return 'character string: \u5b54\u5b50'
                def __str__(self):
            return unicode(self).encode('utf-8')
```

```
    def __str__(self):
        return 'hello'

class TestClass2(object):
    pass
```

Custom Boolean Methods

Custom Boolean methods define a class instance behavior when bool() is called on a class.

In Python 2, we implement the __nonzero__() method to define this behavior.

Download CustomBehaviourOfClasses/booleanpy2.py

```
class test(object):
def __nonzero__(self):
    return False
```

In Python 3, __bool__() replaces __nonzero__().

Download CustomBehaviourOfClasses/booleanp3.py

```
class test(object):
def __bool__(self):
    return False
```

For compatibility, we can just equate __bool__ to __nonzero__.

Download CustomBehaviourOfClasses/soluion1.py

```
class test(object):
def __bool__(self):
    return False
__nonzero__ = __bool__
```

Using Python-future

We can also import future's builtins module and keep the Python 3 syntax.

Download CustomBehaviourOfClasses/future.py

The following is from the builtins import object.

```
class test(object):
def __bool__(self):
    return false
```

Summary

We looked at Python's magic methods: __str__, __nonzero__, __inter__, and next. These methods have different syntax in Python 2 and 3.

We also discussed the compatibility options available in six and future.

TASK: A SIMPLE METHOD

For practice today, your mentor says there is a small method that still uses Python 2's __nonzero__ but your work is to make it compatible. Here is the script.

Download CustomBehaviourOfClasses/task.py

```
class Foo(object):
    def __init__(self):
        self.bar = 3
    def __bool__(self):
        return self.bar > 10
```

He has hidden the correct and compatible script somewhere. Compare your result with the following future option.

Download CustomBehaviourOfClasses/task_future.py

```
from buitlins import object
class Foo(object):
    def __init__(self):
        self.bar = 3
    def __bool__(self):
        return self.bar > 10
```

CHAPTER 10

Collections and Iterators

Python 3 is known to avoid returning lists and dictionaries. If k is a dictionary, in Python 2, k.keys() returns a list of the keys in the dictionary, while in Python 3, k.keys() enables iteration over the keys in something like a for loop. Similarly, k.values() and k.items() returns lists of values or key-value pairs in Python 2, while in Python 3 we can only iterate over the values in a for loop. Python 3 only contains range and it behaves like the Python 2's xrange and in Python 3, the built-in map behaves like Python 2's itertools.imap. Therefore in Python 2 and 3, to get the "old map" behavior, we would instead use list(map(...)). This chapter discusses compatibility for dictionaries, range, and map functions.

Iterable Dictionary Members

I need to mention that there is a difference in how the dict.keys(), dict.values(), and dict.items() operations work between Python 2 and 3. When adapting Python 2 code to Python 3, we get a TypeError when we try to operate on keys(), values(), and items() as lists.

Keys

In Python 3, dict.keys() does not return a list like in Python 2. It instead returns a view *object*. The returned dict_keys object is more like a set than a list. It actually returns iterable keys of a given dictionary.

```
>>> mydict = { 'echo': "lima", 'again': "golf" }
>>> type(mydict .keys())
<class 'dict_keys'>
>>> mydict.keys()
dict_keys(['echo', 'again'])
```

There is a dict.iterkeys() method in Python 2 to return iterable dictionary keys and this method works the same way dict.keys() works. To get iterable keys in both Python 2 and 3, we use six.iterkeys.

Download CollectionsandIterators/six_keys.py

```
import six

mydict = { 'echo': "lima", 'again': "golf" }
for key in six.iterkeys(mydict):
    do_stuff(key)
```

© Joannah Nanjekye 2017
J. Nanjekye, *Python 2 and 3 Compatibility*, https://doi.org/10.1007/978-1-4842-2955-2_10

The `six.iterkeys()` method replaces `dictionary.iterkeys()` in Python 2 and `dictionary.keys()` in Python 3.

There is also another neutral way of getting iterable keys by referring to the dictionary itself. For example, this Python 2 code:

Download CollectionsandIterators/keyspy2.py

```
mydict = { 'echo': "lima", 'again': "golf" }
for key in mydict.iterkeys():
    do_stuff(key)
```

is the same as this:

Download CollectionsandIterators/keyspy2and3.py

```
mydict = { 'echo': "lima", 'again': "golf" }
for key in mydict:
    do_stuff(key)
```

This works in both Python 2 and 3.

In summary, for neutral compatibility for iterable dictionary keys:

- Use `six.iterkeys()`, which replaces `dictionary.keys()` in Python 3 and `dictionary.iterkeys()` in Python 2.

- You can also refer to the dictionary to get iterable keys.

Values

In Python 2, if we want to work with an iterable of dictionary values, then we write code that looks like this:

Download CollectionsandIterators/valuespy2.py

```
mydict = { 'echo': "lima", 'again': "golf" }
for value in heights.itervalues():
    do_stuff(value)
```

We call `itervalues()` in the dictionary. In contrast, in Python 3 we have to call `values()` in the dictionary to achieve the same.

Download CollectionsandIterators/valuespy3.py

```
mydict = { 'echo': "lima", 'again': "golf" }
for value in heights.values():
    do_stuff(value)
```

To support both Python 2 and 3, we have to find a middle ground using one of these options. Use:

- `itervalues()` from six

- `itervalues()` from python-future's builtins module

itervalues() from Python-future's builtins Module

The itervalues() method takes the dictionary as a parameter.

Download CollectionsandIterators/valuesbuiltins.py

```
from builtins import itervalues
mydict = { 'echo': "lima", 'again': "golf" }
for value in itervalues(mydict):
    do_stuff(value)
```

itervalues() from six

Like itervalues() from future's builtins, the itervalues() method from six also takes the dictionary as a parameter and returns iterable values of the dictionary.

Download CollectionsandIterators/values_six.py

```
from six import itervalues
mydict = { 'echo': "lima", 'again': "golf" }
for value in itervalues(mydict):
    do_stuff(value)
```

The itervalues() method replaces dictionary.itervalues() in Python 2 and dictionary.values() in Python 3.

In summary, for neutral compatibility for iterable dictionary values:

- Call six.itervalues() with the dictionary as argument. This replaces dictionary.values in Python 3 and dictionary.itervalues()in Python 2.

- You can also call itervalues() from future's builtins module with the dictionary as argument.

Items

Similarly, dictionary.items() returns a list of dictionary items in Python 2 and dict_item view objects. To get iterable items in Python 2, we use dict.iteritems().

Download CollectionsandIterators/itemspy2.py

```
mydict = { 'echo': "lima", 'again': "golf" }
for (key, value) in heights.iteritems():
    do_stuff(key, value)
```

While in Python 3, we use dict.items().

Download CollectionsandIterators/itemspy3.py

```
mydict = { 'echo': "lima", 'again': "golf" }
for (key, value) in heights.items():
    do_stuff(key, value)
```

There are a couple of ways we can achieve compatibility. future and six have wrappers for this.

iteritems() future Wrapper

We can use the iteritems() method from future to get iterable items. Importing the iteritems module from future overrides Python 2's iteritems() method functionality and Python 3's items() functionality.

Download CollectionsandIterators/items_future.py

```
from future.utils import iteritems

mydict = { 'echo': "lima", 'again': "golf" }
for (key, value) in initeritems(mydict):
    do_stuff(key, value)
```

iteritems() six Wrapper

Similarly, six.iteritems() replaces dictionary.items() in Python 3 and dictionary.iteritems() in Python 2.

Download CollectionsandIterators/items_future.py

```
from future.utils import iteritems

mydict = { 'echo': "lima", 'again': "golf" }
for (key, value) in iteritems(mydict):
    do_stuff(key, value)
```

Dictionary Members as Lists

Keys

In Python 2, we simply use keys() to return a list of keys from a dictionary.

```
>>> mydict = { 'echo': "lima", 'again': "golf" }
>>> type(mydict .keys())
<type 'list'>
>>> mydict .keys()
['echo', 'again']
>>> mydict .keys()[0]
'echo'
```

■ **Note** I said that dict.keys(), dict.values(), and dict.items() return objects which are called view objects. Views are just windows on a dictionary that shows the members of the dictionary even after changes happen to it. A list of members (keys, values) contains a copy of the dictionary members at a given time. Lists do something but views are quite dynamic and are easier and faster to create as we do not have to create a copy of any members (keys, values) to create them.

But as stressed earlier, in Python 3, `dict.keys()` returns an iterable. We can actually reproduce the idea of returning lists in Python 3 by simply casting the returned value to a list.

```
>>> mydict = { 'echo': "lima", 'again': "golf" }
>>> type(list(mydict.keys()))
<class 'list'>
>>> list(mydict .keys())
['echo', 'again']
>>> list(mydict .keys())[0]
'echo'
```

This works well in both Python 2 and 3.

Values

Like keys, `dict.values()` returns a list of values in a dictionary dict.

```
>>> mydict = { 'echo': "lima", 'again': "golf" }
>>> type(mydict .values())
<type 'list'>
>>> mydict .values()
['lima', 'golf']
>>> mydict .values()[0]
'lima'
```

In Python 3, this returns a `dict_values` object.

```
>>> mydict = { 'echo': "lima", 'again': "golf" }
>>> type(mydict .values())
<type 'dict_values'>
```

Compatibility can be maintained by converting the `dict_values` object into a list that can then be indexed as normal in both Python 2 and 3.

Download CollectionsandIterators/values_list.py

```
mydict = { 'echo': "lima", 'again': "golf" }
valuelist = list(mydict.values())
```

This does the work but it has one downside in Python 2. It is very inefficient. Let's discuss similar tricks available to us in six and future.

Using Python-future

Future has a `listvalues()` method from the future.utils module that we should call with the dictionary as argument.

Download CollectionsandIterators/values_list_future1.py

```
from future.utils import listvalues

mydict = { 'echo': "lima", 'again': "golf" }
valuelist = listvalues(mydict)
```

The result is a list of values in the dictionary.

We can also use the itervalues() method from the future.utils module still to get an iterable of the dictionary values.

Download CollectionsandIterators/values_list_future2.py

```
from future.utils import itervalues

mydict = { 'echo': "lima", 'again': "golf" }
values = itervalues(mydict)
valuelist = list(values)
```

Since this method returns an iterable, we should cast its result to a list.

Using six

Like future, six has an itervalues() method that takes the dictionary as argument and returns an iterable of the dictionary values.

Download CollectionsandIterators/values_list_six.py

```
from six import itervalues

mydict = { 'echo': "lima", 'again': "golf" }
values = itervalues(mydict)
valuelist = list(values)
```

Since this method returns an iterable, we should cast its result to a list.

Items

dict.items() returns a list of items in a dictionary dict.

```
>>> mydict = { 'echo': "lima", 'again': "golf" }
>>> type(mydict .items())
<type 'list'>
```

In Python 3, this returns a dict_item object.

```
>>> mydict = { 'echo': "lima", 'again': "golf" }
>>> type(mydict .items()
<type 'dict_items'>
```

For compatibility, convert the dict_items object into a list that can then be indexed as normal in both Python 2 and 3.

Download CollectionsandIterators/items_list.py

```
mydict = { 'echo': "lima", 'again': "golf" }
itemlist = list(mydict.items())
```

This does the work but it has one downside in Python 2. It is also very inefficient. Let's discuss similar tricks available to us by six and future.

Using Python-future

Future has a listitems() method from the future.utils module that we should call with the dictionary as argument.

Download CollectionsandIterators/items_list_future1.py

```
from future.utils import iteritems

mydict = { 'echo': "lima", 'again': "golf" }
itemlist = iteritems(mydict)
```

The result is a list of items in the dictionary.

We can also use the iteritems() method from the future.utils module still to get an iterable of the dictionary items.

Download CollectionsandIterators/items_list_future2.py

```
from future.utils import iteritems

mydict = { 'echo': "lima", 'again': "golf" }
items = iteritems(mydict)
itemlist = list(items)
```

Since this method returns an iterable, we should cast its result to a list.

Using six

Like future, six has an iteritems() method that takes the dictionary as argument and returns an iterable of the dictionary items.

Download CollectionsandIterators/items_list_future2.py

```
from six import iteritems

mydict = { 'echo': "lima", 'again': "golf" }
items = itemitems(mydict)
itemlist = list(items)
```

map

Generally speaking, the map() function applies a given function to each item of an iterable—it may be a list, tuple, and so forth. Depending on the Python version, it returns a different result.

In Python 2, it returns a result that is a list.

Download CollectionsandIterators/map_py2.pp

```
def square(x):
    return x*x

numbers = [1,2,3,4,5,6]
squares = map(square, numbers)
type(squares)          #returns list type
```

In Python 3, the result is not a list but an iterable.

Download CollectionsandIterators/map_py3.pp

```
def square(x):
    return x*x

numbers = [1,2,3,4,5,6]
squares = map(square, numbers)
type(squares)            #returns an iterable
```

The result of the return value is not of type list.

One way we could make use of map and still return the same results in both Python 2 and 3 is to cast the results to lists.

Download CollectionsandIterators/map_alt1.pp

```
def square(x):
    return x*x

numbers = [1,2,3,4,5,6]
squares = list (map(square, numbers))
type(squares)            #returns a list type
```

This returns a result of list type, but it is very inefficient in Python 2.

We can also use optional imports to import itertools.imap as map in a try except block but with nothing in the except block. The module itertools.map does not exist in Python 2.

Download CollectionsandIterators/map_alt2.pp

```
try:
    import itertools.imap as map
except ImportError:
    pass
```

```
def square(x):
    return x*x

numbers = [1,2,3,4,5,6]
squares = map(square, numbers)
type(squares)          #returns a list type
```

This imports itertools.imap as a map, which works well in Python 3 because itertools.imap works the same way map works in Python 2. In Python 2, the import fails since we do not have that module therefore the except block is executed, which we know does nothing thereby executing the default map() function behavior.

Let's discuss the different ways we can achieve compatibility using six and Python-future for the map function.

Using Python-future

Python-future comes with a map method in its builtins module that returns an iterable like in Python 3.

Download CollectionsandIterators/map_future1.py

```
from builtins import map

def square(x):
    return x*x

numbers = [1,2,3,4,5,6]
squares = list (map(square, numbers))
type(squares)          #returns a list type
```

We have to make the result a list.

As another alternative, future offers the lmap() method from the future.utils module. This method returns lists.

Download CollectionsandIterators/map_future2.py

```
from future.utils import lmap

def square(x):
    return x*x

numbers = [1,2,3,4,5,6]
squares = lmap(square, numbers)
type(squares)          #returns a list type
```

Future also has a map() method from the past.builtins module. When used, it returns a result that is a list as intended.

Download CollectionsandIterators/map_future3.py

```
from past.builtins import map

def square(x):
    return x*x

numbers = [1,2,3,4,5,6]
squares = lmap(square, numbers)
type(squares)          #returns a list type
```

Using six

six comes with a map() method from six.moves, which we can call instead of the standard map() function.

Download CollectionsandIterators/map_six.py

```
from six.moves import map

def square(x):
    return x*x

numbers = [1,2,3,4,5,6]
squares = list(map(square, numbers))
type(squares)          #returns a list type
```

This is an equivalent of itertools.imap() in Python 3 and map in Python 2, which both return iterable results. We therefore have to cast the result to a list.

imap

The imap() function applies a given function to each item of an iterable and returns an iterable in Python 2.

Dwnload CollectionsandIterators/imap_py2.py

```
from itertools import imap

def square(x):
    return x*x

numbers = [1,2,3,4,5,6]
squares = imap(square, numbers)
type(squares) #this is an iterable
```

In Python 3, this is deprecated and the same behavior is achievable through the builtin map method.

Dwnload CollectionsandIterators/imap_py2.py

```
def square(x):
    return x*x

numbers = [1,2,3,4,5,6]
squares = map(square, numbers)
type(squares) #this is an iterable
```

To maintain compatibility, we can optionally import Python 2's itertools.imap as map. This returns an iterable in Python 2.

Download CollectionsandIterators/imap_alt1.py

```
try:
    import itertools.imap as map
except ImportError:
    pass

def square(x):
    return x*x

numbers = [1,2,3,4,5,6]
squares = map(square, numbers)
type(squares) #this is an iterable
```

In Python 3, the try block fails, thereby executing the except block, which technically does nothing. This results in executing the builtin map() function, which returns an iterable. This is one of the ways; let's discuss the options we have with six and future.

Using six

six comes with a map() method from six.moves, which we can call instead of the standard map() function as earlier pointed out.

Download CollectionsandIterators/imap_six.py

```
from six.moves import map

def square(x):
    return x*x

numbers = [1,2,3,4,5,6]
squares = map(square, numbers)
type(squares)         #returns a list type
```

This is an equivalent of itertools.imap() in Python 3 and map in Python 2, which both return iterable results.

Using Python-future

Python-future comes with a map method in its builtins module that returns an iterable like in Python 3.

Download CollectionsandIterators/map_future1.py

```
from builtins import map

def square(x):
    return x*x

numbers = [1,2,3,4,5,6]
squares = map(square, numbers)
type(squares)          #returns a list type
```

The result is an iterable in Python 2 and 3.

Range

Both Python 2 and 3 have built-in range functions that return sequences of numbers. The endpoint is not part of the generated sequence.

Python 2, has two functions that generate a sequence of numbers and they include range() and xrange(). The built-in range() function returns a sequence of numbers in a form of a list.

```
>>> range(1,10)
[1, 2, 3, 4, 5, 6, 7, 8, 9]
```

The xrange() function returns an xrange object.

```
>>> type(xrange(10))
<type 'xrange'>
>>>
```

In Python 3, the range() function works the same way xrange() works in Python 2.

```
>>> type(xrange(10))
<type 'xrange'>
>>>
```

For compatibility, we have to stick to using the range() function and casting the result to a list.

Download CollectionsandIterators/range_sol1.py

```
range_list = list(range(5))
assert range_list== [0, 1, 2, 3, 4]
```

Future and six give us a couple of options for compatibility.

Using Python-future

The first option is to use range() function from the builtins module. This function does what Python 3's range does.

Download CollectionsandIterators/range_future1.py

```
from builtins import range
range_list = list(range(5))
assert range_list== [0, 1, 2, 3, 4]
```

> To generate a list of the sequence, we convert the result to list.
> Alternatively, we can use future's lrange() function.

Download CollectionsandIterators/range_future2.py

```
from future.utils import lrange
range_list = lrange(5)
assert range_list == [0, 1, 2, 3, 4]
```

> There is also a range() function from past.builtins that works as Python 2's range function.

Download CollectionsandIterators/range_future2.py

```
from past.builtins import range
range_list = range(5)
assert range_list == [0, 1, 2, 3, 4]
```

Using six

Use six.moves.range to maintain compatibility. This range() function from six generates an iterable object.

Download CollectionsandIterators/range_six.py

```
from six.moves import range
range_iter = range(5)
assert list(range_iter) == [0, 1, 2, 3, 4]
```

> If we want to generate a sequence in list form, then we cast the result to a list.

Summary

This chapter covered dictionaries and the different changes between versions. We saw that items(), keys(), and values() return iterables in Python 3 but lists in Python2. For compatibility, we change the result of these operations to a list. This has efficiency downsides in Python 2; we discussed more efficient ways using six and future.

We also discussed the differences that came with map and imap. imap is deprecated in Python 3, so map does what imap would do. For compatibility, when a result of type list is needed, we cast the result to a list. More cleaner and efficient techniques using six and future were also described.

Finally, we looked at Python 2's range() and xrange() functions. range() generates a result that is a list, whereas xrange() generates iterable results. For portability, use range() and change the generated result to a list. six and future also offer better options using the builtins.range and the six.moves.range.

TASK: CYCLER-MASTER

Project cycler-master has one of its test methods still using Python 2 syntax. Your task is to make this method compatible to both Python 2 and 3.

Download CollectionsandIterators/task.py

```
def test_getitem():
    c1 = cycler(3, xrange(15))
    widths = range(15)
    for slc in (slice(None, None, None),
                slice(None, None, -1),
                slice(1, 5, None),
                slice(0, 5, 2)):
        yield _cycles_equal, c1[slc], cycler(3, widths[slc])
```

Using Python-future this becomes:

Download CollectionsandIterators/task_future.py

```
from builtins import range
def test_getitem():
    c1 = cycler(3, range(15))
    widths = list(range(15))
    for slc in (slice(None, None, None),
                slice(None, None, -1),
                slice(1, 5, None),
                slice(0, 5, 2)):
        yield _cycles_equal, c1[slc], cycler(3, widths[slc])
```

With six, this becomes:

Download CollectionsandIterators/task_six.py

```
from six.moves import range
def test_getitem():
    c1 = cycler(3, range(15))
    widths = list(range(15))
    for slc in (slice(None, None, None),
                slice(None, None, -1),
                slice(1, 5, None),
                slice(0, 5, 2)):
        yield _cycles_equal, c1[slc], cycler(3, widths[slc])
```

## CHAPTER 11

More Built-ins

The previous chapters discussed providing Python 3 support for your existing Python 2 projects, but not everything has been covered. Most of the built-ins were reorganized in Python 3. This chapter looks at other built-in functions and discusses how to achieve compatibility for them.

Reduce

If you have used Python for a while, you may have come across the reduce() function, which is very useful and handy for performing computations on a list of elements and returning the result. It applies a particular function passed in its argument to all the list elements mentioned in the sequence.

Normally, a task like computing the sum of a list integers is achieved using a basic for loop:

Download MoreBuiltins/forloop.py

```
def sum(list):
    sum = 1
    for num in list:
        sum = sum + num

result = sum( [1, 2, 3, 4])
```

The sum() method takes a list of integers and returns their sum. Given the preceding list, the value of the result is 10.

The same functionality can be achieved by using reduce(). In Python 2, reduce() is in the global namespace and used as:

Download MoreBuiltins/reducepy2.py

```
def sum(list):
    sum = reduce((lambda x, y: x + y), list)

result = sum( [1, 2, 3, 4])
```

Calling the sum() method with a list of integers returns the sum of the integers, like the former method that uses a for loop.

■ **Note** The decision to use reduce() or the for loop is yours, but the for loop is easier to read.

Python 3 introduced changes to where the `reduce()` function is located. The function was removed from the global namespace to the functools module. Therefore, for compatibility, use `functools.reduce()`.

Download MoreBuiltins/reducepy2.py

```python
from functools import reduce

def sum(list):
    sum = reduce((lambda x, y: x + y), list)

result = sum( [1, 2, 3, 4])
```

An import is required because `reduce()` is no longer a global function.

■ **Note**   `reduce()` is also available in functools in modern Python 2 versions.

---

six provides a way out through its fake six.moves module. To load the module that has the `reduce()` function in Python 2 and 3, we write:

```python
from six.moves import reduce
```

We can now edit our function using six as:

Download MoreBuiltins/reduce_six.py

```python
from six.moves import reduce

def sum(list):
    sum = reduce((lambda x, y: x + y), list)

result = sum( [1, 2, 3, 4])
```

In this case, the six.moves alias points to the Python 3 module, which is equivalent to calling functools. reduce.

In summary, for Python 2 and 3 compatibility when using `reduce()`:

- Use `functools.reduce()` and not the global `reduce()` function

- Or use six.moves.reduce

raw_input and input

Python 2 has two functions for requesting input from a user: `raw_input()` and `input()`.

`raw_input()` accepts everything given to stdin as a string.

```python
>>> a = raw_input("enter a number :- ")
enter a number :- 4
>>> type(a)
<type 'str'>
```

input(), on the other hand, evaluates the user input as an int or a float, or whatever type it is. Technically, whatever is read from the user is evaluated using eval().

```
>>> a = input("enter a number :- ")
enter a number :- 4
>>> type(a)
<type 'int'>
```

Therefore, input() is the same as eval(raw_input()).

```
>>> a = eval( raw_input("enter a number :- "))
enter a number :- 4
>>> type(a)
<type 'int'>
>>>
```

In Python 3, raw_input() was renamed input(), which now accepts user input in stdin as a string.

```
>>> a = input("enter a number :- ")
enter a number :- 5
>>> type(a)
<class 'str'>
```

raw_input() returns an error in Python 3.

```
>>> a = raw_input("enter a number :- ")
Traceback (most recent call last):
  File "<stdin>", line 1, in <module>
NameError: name 'raw_input' is not defined
>>>
```

We have seen that input() is semantically different in Python 2 and 3, and yet raw_input() is not in Python 3. Both Python-future and six provide wrappers to get around these changes.

Using Python-future

Through its builtins module, Python-future provides a function input that we can use instead of Python 2's raw_ininput(). Therefore, this:

Download MoreBuiltins/input_py2.py

```
first = raw_input("enter first number: ")
second = raw_input("enter second number: ")
print first + second
```

becomes this:

Download MoreBuiltins/input_future.py

```
from builtins import input
first = input("enter first number: ")
second = input("enter second number: ")
print first + second
```

When we use the imported input() method from the builtins module, we get Python 3's behavior in the builtin input() method.

Use eval() on input to achieve Python 2's behavior, where input is evaluated to its respective type.

Download MoreBuiltins/input_eval_future.py

```
from builtins import input
first = eval(input("enter first number: "))
second = eval(input("enter second number: "))
print first + second
```

■ **Note**   eval() has its own dangers when used carelessly. It is not safe to use eval() on strings that you do not trust.

A safe way of parsing user input in a given type is to cast the result to a desired type; for example:

Download MoreBuiltins/input_cast_future.py
from builtins import input

```
first = int(input("enter first number: "))
second = int(input("enter second number: "))
print first + second
```

using six

We can also use six.moves.input(), which points to raw_input() in Python 2 and input() in Python 3.

Download MoreBuiltins/input_future.py

```
from six.moves import input
first = input("enter first number: ")
second = input("enter second number: ")
print first + second
```

In summary, for compatibility when parsing user input

- Use Python future's builtins.input() function

- Optionally use six.moves.input() function

exec()

In Python, exec() executes dynamically created Python code. exec() takes an object that is either a string or an object. A string is parsed as a suite of Python statements, which is then executed. An object is simply executed. You can use the builtin globals() and locals() functions to return the current global and local dictionary, respectively; this may be useful to pass around for use as the second and third argument to exec().

In Python 2, exec is a statement.

Download MoreBuiltins/exec_py2.py

```
globalsParameter = {'__builtins__' : None}
localsParameter = {'print': print, 'dir': dir}
exec 'print(dir())' in globalsParameter, localsParameter
```

In this code, exec is statement used with a keyword when there is need to specify the global and local scopes.

In Python 3, however, exec is a function that is called with the object, global scope, and local scope as optional parameters.

Download MoreBuiltins/exec_py3.py

```
globalsParameter = {'__builtins__' : None}
localsParameter = {'print': print, 'dir': dir}
exec ('print(dir())' , globalsParameter, localsParameter)
```

For compatibility, the best option is to use the Python 3 syntax because it works in Python 2 as well. The other option is to use six.exec_().

Download MoreBuiltins/exec_six.py

```
from math import *

globalsParameter = {'__builtins__' : None}
localsParameter = {'print': print, 'dir': dir}
six.exec_('print(dir())' , globalsParameter, localsParameter)
```

This executes print(dir()) in the scope of *globalParameters* and *localParameters*. print(dir()) is a string in this case. If *globals* or *locals* are not given, they will default to the scope of the caller. If only *globals* is given, it is also used as *locals*.

■ **Note**   In Python 3.x, exec() should not be called with keyword arguments because it does not take keyword arguments.

In summary, when providing compatibility for exec

- Use the Python 3 syntax
- Use six.exec_()

execfile()

In Python 2, execfile() is a function like exec(), but instead of taking a string, it takes a file and the two optional dictionaries as global and local namespaces.

Download MoreBuiltins/execfile_py2.py

```
import sys

sys.argv = ['arg1', 'arg2']
execfile('abc.py')
```

This function was removed in Python 3; therefore, if your existing Python 2 code uses this function, then changes need to be made. Let's discuss how to make these changes.

Using Python-future

From the past.builtins module, we can use the execfile() method, which will do the magic in both Python versions.

Download MoreBuiltins/execfile_future.py

```
from past.builtins import execfile
import sys

sys.argv = ['arg1', 'arg2']
execfile('abc.py')
```

We also have the alternative of using the exec() function along with compile to work with files in this way:

Download MoreBuiltins/execfile_exec_compile.py

```
from past.builtins import execfile
import sys

sys.argv = ['arg1', 'arg2']
execfile(compile(open('abc.py').read()))
```

■ **Note**   At the moment, six does not have a wrapper method for execfile() but there is an open issue requesting for the feature. When someone opens a pull request that solves this issue, then you can use six to go around this compatibility problem; but for now, six has no solution.

In summary, if you use execfile() in your code, then for compatibility

- Use Python-future's execfile() from the past.builtins module
- Use exec() with compile()

Unichr()

In Python 2, `Unichr()` returns the string representation of a character whose Unicode code point is given as argument; for example,

unichr(97)

returns

'a'

The value range that the argument takes is from 1 to 1,114,111. Anything outside this range returns a ValueError.

In Python 3, this method was removed. Instead, use `chr()` to get the string representation of the character, given its Unicode point.

Chr(97)

This also returns

'a'

For compatibility, both six and future have `chr()` and `unichr()` methods.

Using Python-future

Python-future has a `chr()` method from the builtins module that semantically provides the required functionality for both Python versions.

Download MoreBuiltins/unichr_future.py

from builtins import chr

chr(8364)

Using six

six has a `unichr()` method that takes a Unicode point and returns its respective string representation.

Download MoreBuiltins/unichr_six.py

from six import unichr

unichr(8364)

To summarize, for compatibility use

- Python-future's builtins.chr
- six.chr()

Intern()

If you use strings that contain the same characters or text multiple times, then a new string object is created every time. For example,

```
>>> x = "I love chocolate"
>>> y = "I love chocolate"
>>> x is y
False
>>>
```

We end up with two different string objects that have the same value but do not point to the same value. They are then discarded because they're not being used any longer.

On the other hand, if we use interned strings, the intern function saves the strings and returns them from the interned strings table.

```
>>> a = intern("I love chocolate")
>>> b = intern("I love chocolate")
>>> a is b
True
>>>
```

Since the strings *a* and *b* are interned, they now hold the same string object; therefore, *a* is *b* returns *True*. The intern function ensures that we never create two string objects that have the same value. When we try to request the creation of a second string object with the same value as an existing string object, we get a reference to the existing string object. This way, we save memory. In comparison, string objects are very efficient because they are carried out by comparing the memory addresses of the two string objects rather than their content. This is where the intern function helps with performance and optimization in our code.

■ **Note**   Interned strings are technically different from normal strings because they do not allow us to create two string objects that have the same value; whereas strings create two separate objects for the same string.

That is enough about interned strings, but before we go on, I will mention that the intern function in Python 2 is global and therefore used as follows:

Download MoreBuiltins/internpy2.py

```
a = intern ("I love Python")
b = intern ("I love Python")
a is b  # returns True
```

In Python 3, the intern function is not a global function because it was moved to the sys module. Therefore, it is used as follows:

Download MoreBuiltins/internpy2.py

```
from sys import intern
```

```
a = intern ("I love Python")
b = intern ("I love Python")
a is b  # returns True
```

These contrasts can be handled by using optional imports, where we use a try catch block, as follows:

Download MoreBuiltins/intern_optional_import.py

```
try:
    from sys import intern
except ImportError:
    pass

a = intern ("I love Python")
b = intern ("I love Python")
a is b  # returns True
```

In Python 2, the import statement fails when executing the except block, where we actually do nothing. This executes the global intern function. In Python 3, the import in the try block is executed and the intern function from the sys module is used instead. This is just one way. Python-future and six have work arounds for this issue as well.

Using Python-future

One way that future ensures compatibility for the intern function is by availing us with an intern function from its past.builtins module.

Download MoreBuiltins/intern_future_pastbuiltins.py

```
from past. import intern

a = intern ("I love Python")
b = intern ("I love Python")
a is b  # returns True
```

Another way that future provides compatibility for interned strings is through its install_aliases function.

Download MoreBuiltins/intern_future_install_aliases.py

```
install_aliases()

from sys import intern

a = intern ("I love Python")
b = intern ("I love Python")
a is b  # returns True
```

The future package makes the Python 3 sys.intern function available in Python 2.x when we call install_aliases.

Using six

six provides the `six.moves.intern` function to get around the interfunctional differences between Python 2 and 3.

Download MoreBuiltins/intern_six.py

```
from six.moves import intern

a = intern ("I love Python")
b = intern ("I love Python")
a is b  # returns True
```

The `intern` function used is an equivalent of the global `intern` function in Python 2 and the `sys.intern` function in Python 3.

In summary, for compatibility of interned strings

- Import six.moves and use the `intern` function. This is equivalent to `intern` in Python 2 and `sys.intern` in Python 3.

- Call future's `install_aliases` to make Python 3's `sys.intern` function available in Python 2.x

- Import past.builtins and use the `intern` function.

apply

apply is a Python 2 function that basically executes a function. It takes the function and the list of function arguments as parameters.

Download MoreBuiltins/apply_py2.py

```
def add(x, y):
    return x + y

apply (add, [1,2])
```

In Python, this function is obsolete; now, we have to call the function the normal way, as follows:

Download MoreBuiltins/apply_py3.py

```
def add(x, y):
    return x + y

add (1,2)
```

Therefore, if we have Python 2 code that uses the apply method, then we should change it to call the function the normal way, where we call the method and its arguments rather than use apply to execute the function to support Python 3. This saves time and allows faster execution of our program. If you still want to use the apply method, then use Python-future.

■ **Note** The `apply` method is obsolete in Python 3.

Using Python-future

We can keep using the apply function and still support Python 3 when we call the apply function from future's past.builtins module.

Download MoreBuiltins/apply_future.py

```
from past.builtins import apply

def add(x, y):
    return x + y

apply (add, [1,2])
```

This uses the apply function in Python 3.

In summary, to support Python 3 when using the apply function in your Python 2 code

- Change your code to call the method in question normally rather than executing it through the apply function.

- Call future's apply method from the past.builtins module.

chr()

chr() generally takes an integer, which is the Unicode point of a character, and returns a string or characters.

In Python 2.x, chr() converts a number in the range 0–255 to a byte string; one character has the numeric value and unichr(), which converts a number in the 0–0x10FFFF range to a Unicode string with one character with that Unicode codepoint.

Download MoreBuiltins/chr_py2.py

```
chr(64)
chr(200)
```

As discussed earlier, Python 3.x replaces unichr() with chr(). Therefore, to achieve the old chr() functionality, we have two options. One is to encode the result of chr().

Download MoreBuiltins/chr_py3_1.py

```
chr(64).encode('latin-1')
chr(0xc8).encode('latin-1')
```

The other option is to call the global function bytes with the Unicode point of the string that we want to get.

Download MoreBuiltins/chr_py3_2.py

```
bytes([64])
bytes([0xc8])
```

For compatibility, both six and future offer ways to get around these semantical differences. Let's explore each of them.

Using Python-future

One option that future offers is chr() from its builtins module, which uses the same Python 3 syntax as calling chr() and encoding the results.

Download MoreBuiltins/chr_future_1.py

```
from builtins import chr

chr(64).encode('latin-1')
chr(0xc8).encode('latin-1')
```

Alternatively, we can use the bytes method from future's builtins module, which uses same syntax as Python 3's global function bytes.

Download MoreBuiltins/chr_future_2.py

```
from builtins import bytes

bytes([64])
bytes([0xc8])
```

Using six

six provides the int2byte(i) function, which takes an integer in the range (0, 256) and converts or returns it as a byte.

Download MoreBuiltins/chr_six.py

```
from six import int2byte

int2byte(64)
int2byte(0xc8)
```

In summary,

- chr() returns byte strings in Python 2 and in Python 3 it has to be encoded.

- Use Python-future's bytes or chr() methods to get bytes strings.

- We can also use six's Int2byte() method to get byte strings.

cmp()

cmp() is a Python 2 function that compares values; take, for example, two values—a and b.

cmp(a, b)

The result is:

- a negative number if a is less than b.
- zero if a is equal to b.
- a positive number if a is greater than b.

This function is deprecated in Python 3. Let's discuss how to provide Python 3 support for this method.

Using Python-future

We should use the cmp() function from future's past.builtins module.

Download MoreBuiltins/cmp_future.py

```
from past.builtins import cmp

cmp('a', 'b') < 0
cmp('b', 'a') > 0
cmp('c', 'c') == 0
```

This uses the cmp function in Python 3.

reload()

The reload function reloads a previously imported module. This is important when you have edited the module source file using an external editor and want to try out the new version without leaving the Python interpreter. The return value is the module object.

■ **Note**   The argument should be a module that has been successfully imported.

In Python 2, reload() is a global function.

Download MoreBuiltins/reload_py2.py

```
reload(mymodule)
```

In Python 3, the method is to use importlib in versions 3.4 and higher.

Download MoreBuiltins/reload_py3.py

```
from importlib import reload

reload(mymodule)
```

For neutral compatibility, we use `imp.reload`.

Download MoreBuiltins/reload_neutral.py

```
import imp
imp.reload(module)
```

■ **Note**   `imp.reload()` works in Python versions 3.3 and lower. `importlib.reload()` works in Python versions 3.4 and higher.

Summary

This chapter discussed techniques to achieve compatibility for a couple of built-in functions, such as reduce, input, and cmp, among others. Most of these functions have been deprecated, renamed, or reorganized. The remedy to this is future's built-ins package and six's six.moves package.

```
┌─────────────────────────────────────────────────────────────┐
│                    TASK: BAGCAT-MASTER                       │
└─────────────────────────────────────────────────────────────┘
```

The task at hand today is on project bagcat. This project contains a file bagcat.py with a method that still uses Python 2's `raw_input`.

Download MoreBuiltins/task.py

```python
def write_config(args):
    config_file = os.path.join(os.path.expanduser("~"), '.bagcat')
    if os.path.isfile(config_file):
        if raw_input("overwrite existing %s [Y/N] " % config_file).upper() != "Y":
            return
    config = configparser.RawConfigParser()
    for name in ['aws_access_key_id', 'aws_secret_access_key', 'bucket']:
        value = raw_input("%s: " % name)
        config.set('DEFAULT', name, value)
    config.write(open(config_file, 'w'))
```

Let's see what this code looks like when made compatible.

Using Python-future

As discussed, use `input()` from the builtins package.

Download MoreBuiltins/task_future.py

```python
from builtins import input
def write_config(args):
    config_file = os.path.join(os.path.expanduser("~"), '.bagcat')
    if os.path.isfile(config_file):
```

```
        if input("overwrite existing %s [Y/N] " % config_file).upper() != "Y":
            return
    config = configparser.RawConfigParser()
    for name in ['aws_access_key_id', 'aws_secret_access_key', 'bucket']:
        value = input("%s: " % name)
        config.set('DEFAULT', name, value)
    config.write(open(config_file, 'w'))
```

Using six

As with Python-future, use `input()` from six.moves.

Download MoreBuiltins/task_six.py

```
from six.moves import input
def write_config(args):
    config_file = os.path.join(os.path.expanduser("~"), '.bagcat')
    if os.path.isfile(config_file):
        if input("overwrite existing %s [Y/N] " % config_file).upper() != "Y":
            return
    config = configparser.RawConfigParser()
    for name in ['aws_access_key_id', 'aws_secret_access_key', 'bucket']:
        value = input("%s: " % name)
        config.set('DEFAULT', name, value)
    config.write(open(config_file, 'w'))
```

CHAPTER 12

■ ■ ■

Standard Library Modules

The Python standard library was reorganized to make it easier and consistent. Many of the modules were renamed to conform to PEP 8 and unify file-naming conventions. Others merged to put related modules in a common namespace. This chapter explores some of the renamed and reorganized modules and explains how to provide compatibility for them.

Tkinter

If you have tried creating programs using a graphical user interface, then you have come across Tkinter. It is a standard library module that functions as an interface to Tk, a small toolkit.

The module is called Tkinter in Python 2 but it was renamed tkinter in Python 3 (the difference is in the capitalization of the first letter).

Other modules related to GUI development were removed from the global namespace and placed in the tkinter namespace. Table 12-1 lists these modules.

Table 12-1. *Tkinter Namespace Modules*

Python 2	Python 3
Dialog	tkinter.dialog
FileDialog	tkinter.filedialog
ScrolledText	Tkinter.scrolledtext
SimpleDialog	tkinter.simpledialog
Tix	tkinter.tix
Tkconstants	tkinter.constants
Tkdnd	tkinter.dnd
tkColorChooser	tkinter.clorchooser
tkCommonDialog	tkinter.commondialog
tkFileDialog	tkinter.filedialog
tkFont	tkinter.font
tkMessageBox	tkinter.messagebox
tkSimpleDialog	tkinter.simpledialog
ttk	tkinter.ttk

© Joannah Nanjekye 2017

J. Nanjekye, *Python 2 and 3 Compatibility*, https://doi.org/10.1007/978-1-4842-2955-2_12

Python-future and six provide wrappers to maintain compatibility where the Tkinter module has been used in the code base. The following is Python 2 source code with Tkinter imports:

Download MoreBuiltins/tkinter_py2.py

```
import Tkinter
import Dialog
import FileDialog
import ScrolledText
import SimpleDialog
import Tix
import Tkconstants
import Tkdnd
import tkColorChooser
import tkCommonDialog
import tkFileDialog
import tkFont
import tkMessageBox
import tkSimpleDialog
import ttk
```

Using Python-future

In Python-future, the preceding Tkinter modules can be implemented as follows:

Download MoreBuiltins/tkinter_future.py

```
import tkinter
import tkinter.dialog
import tkinter.filedialog
import tkinter.scrolledtext
import tkinter.simpledialog
import tkinter.tix
import tkinter.constants
import tkinter.dnd
import tkinter.colorchooser
import tkinter.commondialog
import tkinter.filedialog
import tkinter.font
import tkinter.messagebox
import tkinter.simpledialog
import tkinter.ttk
```

These future wrappers call the right tkinter module in Python 2 and 3.

Using six

Through its six.moves module, six exposes all the renamed and exposed modules in a name that is compatible with both Python 2 and 3.

Download MoreBuiltins/tkinter_future.py

```
from six.moves import tkinter

from six.moves  import dialog
from six.moves import filedialog
from six.moves import scrolledtext
from six.moves import simpledialog
from six.moves import tix
from six.moves import constants
from six.moves import dnd
from six.moves import colorchooser
from six.moves import commondialog
from six.moves import filedialog
from six.moves import font
from six.moves import messagebox
from six.moves import simpledialog
from six.moves import .ttk
```

The recommended fixer changes imports to use `six.moves`.

Configparser

Configparser is a Python module that works with configuration files. It has many similarities with Windows INI files. It handles user-editable configuration files for any application. Configuration files are organized into sections, and each section can contain name-value pairs of configuration data. Configuration file sections are identified by looking for lines that start with [and end with]. A typical configuration file looks like this:

Download StandardLibraryModules/sample_config.py

```
[AWS_main]
endpoint = https://www.amazon.com/
accesskey = mdl;ldklsld
secretkey = fkndjfdgkdfhsdfj
```

In Python 2, this module is called Configparser (with an uppercase first letter; therefore this is how it is used).

Download StandardLibraryModules/configparser_py2.py

```
from ConfigParser import ConfigParser

ConfigParser.SafeConfigParser()
```

This module was renamed.

Download StandardLibraryModules/configparser_py2.py

```
from configparser import ConfigParser

configparser.ConfigParser()
```

From this example, we see that the SafeConfigParser function was renamed ConfigParser in Python 3. To work around these differences and maintain compatibility, use six.moves or the configparser backport.

Using configparser Backport

The configparser backport is PyPi installable package installed using pip install configparser. Installing this package, importing it in your code, and using the Python 3 renamed modules works on both Python versions.

Download StandardLibraryModules/configparser_backport.py

```
from configparser. import ConfigParser

configparser.ConfigParser()
```

Using six.moves

From the six.moves module, import configparser, which works well for both Python 2 and 3.

Download StandardLibraryModules/configparser_six.py

```
import six

from six.moves import configparser

configparser.ConfigParser()
```

In summary, for compatibility when reading and writing config files:

- Install and use the backported configparser
- Use the six.moves.configparser

Queue

The Queue module implements queues to aid with multiple-thread programming. The Python Queue object can be used to solve the multi-producer, multi-consumer problem where messages have to be exchanged safely between and among multiple threads. The locking semantics have been implemented in the Queue class; therefore, there is no need to handle the low-level lock and unlock operations, which may cause deadlock problems.

The Queue module was renamed to "queue" in Python 3; therefore, if you wanted to use this module in Python 2:

Download StandardLibraryModules/queue_py2.py

```
from Queue import  Queue
```

It would be this in Python 3:

Download StandardLibraryModules/queue_py3.py

```
from queue import  Queue
```

By using six and Python-future, we can import the synchronized queue class that is compatible with both Python 2 and 3.

Using Python-future

In Python-future, we import a single queue class that functions reliably in both Python versions.

Download StandardLibraryModules/queue_future.py

```
from queue import  Queue
```

Using six

Like Python-future, six features single queue classes that we can use to ensure compatibility in both Python 2 and 3.

Download StandardLibraryModules/queue_six.py

```
import six
from six.moves.queue import  Queue, heapq, deque
```

In summary, import the synchronized queue class for compatibility using

- queue from Python-future
- six.moves.queue

socketserver

The socketserver module is a framework that simplifies the creation of network servers. It features classes that handle synchronous network requests over TCP, UDP, Unix streams, and Unix datagrams. Depending on what is appropriate, it also provides classes that convert servers to use a separate thread or process for every request.

The socketserver module has five different server classes defined in it; BaseServer defines the API. This class should never be instantiated, even if used directly. TCPServer uses TCP/IP sockets to communicate. UDPServer uses datagram sockets. UnixStreamServer and UnixDatagramServer use Unix-domain sockets.

115

In Python 2, the socketserver module is spelled "SocketServer"—using camel case letters.

Download StandardLibraryModules/socketserver_py2.py

```python
import SocketServer

class MyTCPHandler(socketserver.BaseRequestHandler):

    def handle(self):
        # self.request is the TCP socket connected to the client
        self.data = self.request.recv(1024).strip()
        print("{} wrote:".format(self.client_address[0]))
        print(self.data)
        # just send back the same data, but upper-cased
        self.request.sendall(self.data.upper())

if __name__ == "__main__":
    HOST, PORT = "localhost", 9999

    # Create the server, binding to localhost on port 9999
    server = socketserver.TCPServer((HOST, PORT), MyTCPHandler)
    server.serve_forever()
```

In Python 3, this module was changed and renamed to "socketserver"—all lowercase letters.

Download StandardLibraryModules/socketserver_py2.py

```python
import socketserver

class MyTCPHandler(socketserver.BaseRequestHandler):

    def handle(self):
        # self.request is the TCP socket connected to the client
        self.data = self.request.recv(1024).strip()
        print("{} wrote:".format(self.client_address[0]))
        print(self.data)
        # just send back the same data, but upper-cased
        self.request.sendall(self.data.upper())

if __name__ == "__main__":
    HOST, PORT = "localhost", 9999

    # Create the server, binding to localhost on port 9999
    server = socketserver.TCPServer((HOST, PORT), MyTCPHandler)
    server.serve_forever()
```

For compatibility in both Python 2 and 3, Python-future provides the socketserver module, and six provides the moves.socketserver module to get around these differences.

Using Python-future

If you pip-installed Python-future, then you should have access to Python-future's socketsever module, which you can import and use.

Download StandardLibraryModules/socketserver_future.py

```
import socketserver

class MyTCPHandler(socketserver.BaseRequestHandler):

    def handle(self):
        # self.request is the TCP socket connected to the client
        self.data = self.request.recv(1024).strip()
        print("{} wrote:".format(self.client_address[0]))
        print(self.data)
        # just send back the same data, but upper-cased
        self.request.sendall(self.data.upper())

if __name__ == "__main__":
    HOST, PORT = "localhost", 9999

    # Create the server, binding to localhost on port 9999
    server = socketserver.TCPServer((HOST, PORT), MyTCPHandler)
    server.serve_forever()
```

Much as the module name imported is the Python 3 one, without installing future then this code will not work on Python 2.

Using six

In six.moves, we can import and use the socketserver module.

Download StandardLibraryModules/socketserver_six.py

```
from six.moves import socketserver

class MyTCPHandler(socketserver.BaseRequestHandler):

    def handle(self):
        # self.request is the TCP socket connected to the client
        self.data = self.request.recv(1024).strip()
        print("{} wrote:".format(self.client_address[0]))
        print(self.data)
        # just send back the same data, but upper-cased
        self.request.sendall(self.data.upper())
```

```
if __name__ == "__main__":
    HOST, PORT = "localhost", 9999

    # Create the server, binding to localhost on port 9999
    server = socketserver.TCPServer((HOST, PORT), MyTCPHandler)
    server.serve_forever()
```

In summary, to maintain compatibility when using the socketserver module, import

- socketserver from Python-future

- socketserver from six.moves

dbm Modules

Python features a database API that is very beneficial when working with different types of databases. The data is stored in a database manager known as DBM. At its core, persistent dictionaries function the same way normal Python dictionaries do, except that data is written and read from a disk.

There are many DBM modules that are not compatible. In Python 2, some of these modules are used as follows:

Download StandardLibraryModules/dbmmodule_py2.py

```
import anydbm
import whichdb
import dbm
import dumbdbm
import gdbm
```

In Python 3, these modules were restructured and moved to a submodule DBM.

Download StandardLibraryModules/dbmmodule_py3.py

```
import dbm.anydbm
import dbm.whichdb
import dbm.dbm
import dbm.dumbdbm
import dbm.gdbm
```

The difference is the submodule, where the modules were moved to because they do not exist in Python 2. Let's see how we can use Python-future and six to bring balance to the source.

Using Python-future

Using Python-future, we can import the standard_library module, call the install_aliases() method, and thereafter use the Python 3 syntax.

Download StandardLibraryModules/dbmmodule_future1.py

```
from future import standard_library
standard_library.install_aliases()
```

```
import dbm
import dbm.ndbm
import dbm.dumb
import dbm.gnu
```

Alternatively, we can import these modules from future.moves.

Download StandardLibraryModules/dbmmodule_future2.py

```
from future.moves import dbm
from future.moves.dbm import dumb
from future.moves.dbm import ndbm
from future.moves.dbm import gnu
```

Using six

six provides the DBM's gnu module; but at the time this book was written, it did not provide support for the other incompatible modules.

Download StandardLibraryModules/dbmmodule_six.py

```
from six.moves import dbm_gnu
```

http Module

This module defines classes that handle the client side of the HTTP and HTTPS protocols. Most of the modules handling HTTP were moved to a package HTTP.

In Python 2, the HTTP modules were accessed globally for use, like this:

Download StandardLibraryModules/http_py2.py

```
import httplib
import Cookie
import cookielib
import BaseHTTPServer
import SimpleHTTPServer
import CGIHttpServer
```

In Python 3, these modules were reorganized; modules such as BaseHTTPServer are in http.server.

Download StandardLibraryModules/http_py3.py

```
import http.client
import http.cookies
import http.cookiejar
import http.server
```

For compatibility, we can use either Python-future or six to bring balance.

Using Python-future

After pip installs future, the respective Python 3 syntax should work reliably in both Python versions.

Download StandardLibraryModules/http_future.py

```
import http.client
import http.cookies
import http.cookiejar
import http.server
```

Using six

In the six.moves package, we can also import these modules and have them work well in both Python 2 and 3.

Download StandardLibraryModules/http_future.py

```
from six.moves import http.client
from six.moves  import http.cookies
from six.moves  import http.cookiejar
from six.moves import http.server
```

XML-RPC

XML-RPC is a *remote procedure call* method that uses XML passed via HTTP as a transport.[1] A client can therefore call methods with parameters on a remote server to get structured data.

In Python 2, there are two modules—DocXMLRPCServer and SimpleXMLRPCServer—and xmlrpclib to handle server and client XML-RPC.

Download StandardLibraryModules/xmlrpc_py2.py

```
# for servers
import DocXMLRPCServer
import SimpleXMLRPCServer

# for clients
import xmlrpclib
```

The preceding modules are all organized in a single package, xmlrpc, which contains two modules to handle xmlrpc for clients and servers, respectively.

Download StandardLibraryModules/xmlrpc_py3.py

```
import xmlrpc.client
import xmlrpc.server
```

After pip installs future, we can use the Python 3 syntax, which works reliably in both Python 2 and Python 3.

Download StandardLibraryModules/xmlrpc_future.py

```
import xmlrpc.client
import xmlrpc server
```

ifilterfalse

By definition, ifilterfalse returns those items of sequence for which function(item) is false. If the function is None, it returns the items that are false. This function was renamed filterfalse in Python 3. To maintain compatibility, we will use either Python-future or six, as follows.

Using six

Import and use the renamed value; that is, use filterfalse instead of ifilterfalse.

Download StandardLibraryModules/filterfalse_six.py

```
from six.moves import filterfalse

list=[1,2,3,4,5]
list(itertools.filterfalse(filterfalse, list))
```

Using future

As with six, import and use filterfalse from future.moves.itertools.

Download StandardLibraryModules/filterfalse_six.py

```
from future.moves.itertools import filterfalse
list=[1,2,3,4,5]
list(itertools.filterfalse(filterfalse, list)
```

izip_longest

izip_longest was renamed zip_longest in Python 3; therefore, for compatibility, use the six or future options.

Using six

Import and use the renamed value; that is, use zpl_longest instead of iziplongest.

Download StandardLibraryModules/filterfalse_six.py

```
from six.moves import zip_longest

def solve(seq):
      sentinel = object()
      return [tuple(x for x in item if x is not sentinel) for item zip_longest(*seq,
      fillvalue=sentinel)]
```

Using future

As with six, import and use zip_longest from future.moves.itertools.

Download StandardLibraryModules/filterfalse_six.py

```
from future.moves.itertools import zip+longest
def solve(seq):
      sentinel = object()
      return [tuple(x for x in item if x is not sentinel) for item zip_longest(*seq,
      fillvalue=sentinel)]
```

UserDict, UserList and UserString

If we want to import these modules in Python 2, then we import them from separate packages.

Download StandardLibraryModules/user_py2.py

```
from UserDict import UserDict
from UserList import UserList
from UserString import UserString
```

In Python 3, they are all reorganized to a common package called collections; therefore, we import them as follows:

Download StandardLibraryModules/user_py3.py

```
from collections import UserDict, UserList, UserString
```

```
For compatibility, we will use future or six.
```

Using six

Import them from the common six.moves package.

```
from six.moves import UserDict, UserList, UserString
```

Using future

Import them from the future.moves.collections package.

```
from future.moves.collections import UserDict, UserList, UserString
```

Copy_reg

The copy_reg module in Python 2 provides a registry to register our own extension types.

Download StandardLibraryModules/copy_reg_py2.py

```
import copy_reg

def test_class(self):
        self.assertRaises(TypeError, copy_reg.pickle, C, None, None)
```

This module was renamed to copyreg in Python 3.

Download StandardLibraryModules/copy_reg_py.py

```
import copyreg

def test_class(self):
        self.assertRaises(TypeError, copyreg.pickle, C, None, None)
```

For compatibility, use future or six, as shown next.

Using six

Import the module from six.moves.

Download StandardLibraryModules/copy_reg_six.py

```
From six.moves import copyreg

def test_class(self):
        self.assertRaises(TypeError, copyreg.pickle, C, None, None)
```

Using future

Import copyreg after pip installs future, and it will work reliably in both Python 2 and 3.

Download StandardLibraryModules/copy_reg_future.py

```
import copyreg

def test_class(self):
        self.assertRaises(TypeError, copyreg.pickle, C, None, None)
```

Summary

This chapter discussed the techniques to achieve compatibility for a couple of standard library functions like socketserver, zip_longest, and so forth. Most of the functions are deprecated, renamed, or reorganized. The remedy to this is given by Python-future's built-ins package and six's six.moves package.

TASK: PYTHON-JENKINS

Today, your task is from a project called Python-jenkins. The project is in the helper.py file with an incompatible `init` method.

Download StandardLibraryModules/task.py

```
def __init__(self, server_address, *args, **kwargs):
    # TCPServer is old style in python 2.x so cannot use
    # super() correctly, explicitly call __init__.

    # simply init'ing is sufficient to open the port, which
    # with the server not started creates a black hole server
    socketserver.TCPServer.__init__(
        self, server_address, socketserver.BaseRequestHandler,
        *args, **kwargs)
```

With a couple of edits, the compatible version of this code looks like the following.

Using six

Use socketserver module from six.moves.

Download StandardLibraryModules/task_six.py

```
from six.moves import socketserver

def __init__(self, server_address, *args, **kwargs):
    # TCPServer is old style in python 2.x so cannot use
    # super() correctly, explicitly call __init__.

    # simply init'ing is sufficient to open the port, which
    # with the server not started creates a black hole server
    socketserver.TCPServer.__init__(
        self, server_address, socketserver.BaseRequestHandler,
        *args, **kwargs)
```

Using future

Use socketserver module from future.

Download StandardLibraryModules/task_future.py

```
import socketserver

def __init__(self, server_address, *args, **kwargs):
    # TCPServer is old style in python 2.x so cannot use
    # super() correctly, explicitly call __init__.

    # simply init'ing is sufficient to open the port, which
    # with the server not started creates a black hole server
    socketserver.TCPServer.__init__(
        self, server_address, socketserver.BaseRequestHandler,
        *args, **kwargs)
```

Index

Get the eBook for only $5!

Why limit yourself?

With most of our titles available in both PDF and ePUB format, you can access your content wherever and however you wish—on your PC, phone, tablet, or reader.

Since you've purchased this print book, we are happy to offer you the eBook for just $5.

To learn more, go to http://www.apress.com/companion or contact support@apress.com.

Apress®